From reading this book you will learn:

- about unique places to search for assets known and accessible only to a select few based on our experience

- to identify and analyze properties to choose the best option for investment

- the negotiation process and be able to develop skills to negotiate transaction successfully to maximize your benefits

- how to get the best price and contractors for repairs for your project

- how to maximize the profits, minimize your risks while disposing of your properties much quicker than your competitors

- how and where to connect with like-minded individuals to support your vision, growth, and development

- to eliminate negative influences from your environment and much more

"Knowledge is power when applied with action to a plan for a specific outcome."

~ *Richard C. Phipps*

Praise for

Genuine Real Estate Investing Made Easy

As an educator, I had the opportunity to work with many individuals across many races, ethnic groups and income and education levels. Some years ago, I came to know the author of this book both through the educational process as a student and later through a real estate transaction. He is a wealth of knowledge and unique experiences who seems never to have a dull or down moment. He eats, sleeps and breaths real estate 24/7. I don't believe that I have met anyone equal or better. He has been a source of inspiration and encouragement and you will probably find that he does the same for you as a reader, a student, or mentee. He is the real deal.

~ Emmanuel Allen
Boston Public School Reengagement Center Manager

I had the opportunity and honor to work with Mr. Phipps and I am deeply in awe of the quality of person he is. He has accomplished much with family, society, and mainly business. His drive for excellence in those areas made his remarkable ability to inspire and mentor people to excel in the business. The book offers insights to guide you in your journey of real estate investing. The dissection of details are made simple because of the information laid out in this book. There are checklists, reminders, cautions, and I found the chapter that includes "Taking Time to Learn the Ropes" section alone to be invaluable. Whether a first time buyer, seller or a seasoned agent or investor, this book will quickly become your go-to source for all things real estate. Reading this book is essential before plunging into one of the biggest investments of a lifetime!

~ Geralyn Cando-Suazo, Philippines, Asia

I started my career as a civil engineer out of North Eastern University Boston. After years of excellent performance, I was released from the company that I thought could not operate without me because I could not advance beyond the owner. I decided that I will not allow that to happen again and became an entrepreneur as a personal financial analyst helping individuals to make wise choices about their future and finances. During this period, I had the opportunity to work with the author of this book whose keen insight, knowledge of the real estate marketplace both local and national and his passion for the business of real estate far surpassed anyone else I have ever dealt with. He always has the interest of the other people first. He is an unbelievable individual and now a dear friend who I hold in very high regard. He is trustworthy and a man of his word. His knowledge, experience, and guidance will serve you well as you pursue developing a financial plan for your future especially as it relate to your real estate investments and options.

~ Jesus Sanoja, PFS, Sr. VP

Genuine
Real Estate
Investing
Made Easy

Net proceeds from the sale of each book will be distributed to support the charitable causes listed below:

• First time homebuyer education programs/down payment assistance • Post high school academic scholarships or university/ college academic scholarships • NAREB programs as designated • Children with physical disabilities •

Genuine
Real Estate
Investing
Made Easy

PROVEN STRATEGIES FOR LOW RISK & HIGH PROFIT OPPORTUNITIES

Richard C. Phipps

Foreword by Senator Gerald A. Neal

Richard C. Phipps
150 Belgrade Avenue
Roslindale, MA 02131
(617) 296-7730
RCPhipps@GMail.com
http://cfsrealty.com/agents/richard-phipps/
http://GenuineRealEstateInvestingMadeEasy.com

ISBN-13: 978-09986563-2-8

ISBN-10: 09986563-2-1

Limits of Liability and Disclaimer of Warranty
The author and publisher shall not be liable for your misuse of this material. This book is strictly for informational and educational purposes.

Warning–Disclaimer

The purpose of this book is to educate and entertain. The author and/or publisher do not guarantee that anyone following these techniques, suggestions, tips, ideas, or strategies will become successful. The author and/or publisher shall have neither liability nor responsibility to anyone with respect to any loss or damage caused, or alleged to be caused, directly or indirectly by the information contained in this book.

Cover images: Used in accordance with Pixabay.com Terms & Conditions, released free of copyrights under Creative Commons CC0.

Interior images: Used in accordance with DepositPhotos.com Terms & Conditions, purchased under a royalty-free license, within the bounds stated by the Standard or Extended licenses.

Table of Contents

In Gratitude

This book is written with collaborative effort from several folks of whom I wish to mention.

First and foremost I would like to thank my lovely wife, Cheryl, for her support while having this crazy idea to write a book. I would also like to extend that same appreciation to my children Erika, Michelle, Kimberly, Shavon, Shavonne, Candice, Richard R., Sade, Helena, Amber, and TJ, all of whom have been direct inspiration for the writing of this book.

Next I would like to offer my deepest appreciation and gratitude to my assistant, Geralyn Cando. She not only is my eyes but my right hand as well.

I would also like to extend a special thanks to an individual whom I've admired for many years and who has not only supported but guided me to many of my learning curves with great discipline, Ron Rainer.

Many thanks to Irvin Whitlow, whose commitment to real estate investing as a way to serve community coupled with his many trials as a landlord and property owner provided many lessons over the years which made the writing of this book even more important as a guide to avoid pitfalls.

To Atty. David Hadlock, whose wealth of experience as a Compliance Attorney enabled the development of versatile funding programs to serve the needs of our network of aspiring investors whenever and wherever possible.

I would also like to extend a heartfelt gratitude to the CFS real estate team for all their love and support through the process.

Thanks to the many students who have given me the privilege and entrusted me with the opportunity to teach and coach them into careers as successful real estate professionals and investors.

Also, sincere thanks to my good friend Gerald Neal who so graciously agreed to write the Foreword without hesitation.

To my editor, Peggy Lee Hanson who assisted with this book every step along the way. I could not have done this without her.

Last but not least, sincere gratitude to my wonderful parents Richard E. Phipps and Muriel Ione Phipps posthumously for their love, guidance, and expectation of excellence.

Mere thanks does not do justice to the gratitude I feel in my heart.

"For example, who of you wanting to build a tower does not first sit down and calculate the expense to see if he has enough to complete it? Otherwise, he might lay its foundation but not be able to finish it, and all the onlookers would start to ridicule him, saying: 'This man started to build but was not able to finish.'"

~ *Luke 14:28-30 (NWT)*

Foreword

Real Estate plays a vital role in our economy. The dollar volume for the real estate transactions in the U.S. economy range from 215 billion dollars in 2004 to 430 billion in 2014 according to Prof. Dr. Matthias Thomas, author of Property Finance. The foundation of its powerful economic impact is the fact that real estate is the key to the wealth of most people, especially for many homeowners in the United States. This is reflected in the most recent Federal Reserve Survey of Consumer Finances. Real Estate constitutes 65.2% of the wealth of American families in the form of their primary residence. The size and scope of the real estate market is exactly what makes it such an attractive business opportunity, and why this book by Richard C. Phipps entitled, "Genuine Real Estate Investing Made Easy," is so timely.

Richard C. Phipps, founder of CFS Realty and Management and Consumer Financial Services brings his 35 plus years of experience in the real estate industry, and explains the key steps and perspectives that must be understood in order to invest in this marketplace successfully. His comprehensive background in several areas of management, marketing, and sales, as they relate to finance and real estate, is the underpinning of his approach to the subject. His comprehensive background supported by extensive research and analysis is presented here in simple, understandable terms for you to follow a path that enhances your opportunity to successfully enter this line of endeavor.

Mr. Phipps started his journey in financial services in 1977 and added real estate to his portfolio of activities shortly thereafter. He currently serves as Regional VP of National Association of Real Estate Brokers (NAREB), Region 1 the New England State. He works diligently in this capacity to advance the cause of democracy and housing for all. He's produced numerous successful brokers and agents during his career and enjoys supporting their continuing efforts. He also has extensive experience in counseling services.

It is estimated that the industry supports more than 421,300 jobs, and in addition more than 400,000 agents and brokers selling approximately 5,250,000 homes representing $430 billion as part of the U.S. Gross Domestic Product (GDP). The real estate agent broker pool of professionals is expected to grow by 3.5% by 2024.

According to the Bureau of Labor Statistics' most recent 2014 information, the real estate industry employs over 2 million people in addition to the agents and brokers. This represents 1.4% of the working civilian population of the United States. A great deal of the cash flow derives from real estate investments, both long term and short term, and the diverse sources that it represents, provides many institutional hedge funds, pension funds, and ordinary citizens across the U.S. with the sense of economic security and inclusion in the real estate market place. In recent years, the total revenue for the real estate industry was greater than the GDPs of Australia, United Kingdom, and Russia, together.

The opportunity is apparent to individuals interested in pursuing areas of the real estate industry for profits, financial independence, wealth development, and other options for satisfaction.

This unique and engaging book blends theory and practice in a simple, and easy to understand tool to start on your road to success. The only ingredient needed for success, with the knowledge and experience offered here, is your effort, passion, and focus on the goal you would like to achieve.

All the best,

Senator Gerald A. Neal
Kentucky State Senate, District 33

Genuine

Real Estate Investing

Made Easy

~ 1 ~

The World Within

You have this friend—we'll call him Joe—who is in real estate. Joe is not just in real estate; he is a real estate investor, REI for short. Not knowing what that may mean, exactly—yet you see Joe as successful; for he has a beautiful house, a big boat, and travels around the world at whim, or so it seems—you wonder what that world is like, truly. You may also wonder, after seeing what Joe has accomplished and acquired, if becoming a real estate investor could work for you, too.

ABCs of REI

Real estate investing is the real deal. It can be done as a hobby or as a business, full-time or part-time, in the field or from the comfort of your home; individually or with partners; in your hometown or out of town; with no money, your money, or someone else's money.

Investment opportunities could be residential, commercial, industrial, agricultural, or a combination of them all or just some of them—provided you have the knowledge, experience, and capability to execute what could be called a successful real estate transaction.

Even if you are not yet experienced in the REI areas of skill, knowledge, or experience to complete a deal, it is conceivable that you could be able to find someone with those components you lack to augment the transaction that ensures its success—otherwise known as partnering.

You may be asking, "I don't need any experience or knowledge to do what Joe does?"

Individuals enter into the game of real estate investing lifestyle from different paths, yet, very seldom is it accidental.

In conversations with REIs, there have been several reasons given as to why they entered into the pursuit of real estate investing happiness.

For many, it was the excitement of the hunt for the best, great deal. For some, it was a lifelong passion to be in the real estate profession. And for others, it is making enormous sums of money when applying accurate knowledge in the REI arena. There are also a few that were drawn in by a friend who was afraid of entering that realm by themselves.

Whatever your reason may be to get into the real estate investment arena, you've chosen what can be both an exciting and challenging profession, which has the potential for significant profit. With that said, be mindful that where there is the possibility of great reward, there is also great risk.

It is my expectation and profound wish, that as you continue to read this book, you will find nuggets of information, various formulas, and expert guidance to keep you on the positive side of the profit equation—all while in the midst of the acquisition and disposition process of real estate investments.

This book offers genuine and honest advice to help you develop the insight necessary to make good judgment calls and exercise wisdom in your decision-making processes when acquiring (buying) and disposing of (selling) property.

There are no guarantees in life. However, if you follow a successful model it should lead you to profitability as you exercise timeliness and the application and use of the resources and tools herein provided.

As long as you are consistent and follow a plan, you can practice real estate investing anywhere in the United States—and for that matter, in the world. But that is beyond the scope of this book. It is best to start in an area with which you are familiar. You must also develop or have vast knowledge about the market and the assets in that market.

What You Need to Know Upfront about REI

Many people have an interest in learning about real estate investing. You are one of them. I know this because you are here. Investing in real estate is one of the most secure ways to gain profits and cash flow, or liquidity. Observers marvel at the wealth created and displayed by many of those who have had great success in the industry.

You may wonder what enables or helps individuals to be successful in real estate investing. What does make the difference between those who have succeeded in buying and selling or renting large numbers of property and those who have not yet been able to acquire a home of their own versus investment properties? The answers are forthcoming.

A Bit of My Story

Frequently I'm asked how I started investing in real estate.

In May 1979 I bought a lovely, three-bedroom, single-family house that I thought was a mansion. At the time I was serving in the military at Nellis, Nevada, about thirty minutes away from where I lived. About a year later, I wanted to move closer to the base, so I sold the house. The profit made from that sale, and after only one year of owning the home was very exciting! As a matter of fact, my military wage was about one thousand dollars per month, and when I received the check from the closing, I thought I could retire on that profit alone! It was at that point I started to fall in love with the real estate business. No wonder, right?

I continued to own several properties in Las Vegas, and over time, all sold for more than I spent to acquire them. Making money and keeping it, however, requires two different skill sets, and at that time in my life, I did not have the money management skill set to keep what I made. You can imagine what happened to the dollars.

Process Overview

Let us consider a few steps that could help anyone with the desire to become a real estate investor. You will find this process a familiar theme throughout this book.

◊ Stick to the Plan

I started with the idea to purchase a home which I could afford to accommodate my family, with the intent to relocate whenever the family grew from three to four, which, naturally, did not take long. It is, therefore, essential that you adhere to the plan when acquiring and disposing of—or using—your acquisitions.

◊ Start at Home

Although you can invest in real estate anywhere, it makes DOLLARS and CENTS to begin in your immediate backyard. Being familiar with the territory is one way to eliminate some of the fear you could experience from being in an unfamiliar area. This anxiety can impede a new investor from getting started on the right path to success. Therefore, stay close to home and do not adventure into the town down the road, for instance, to begin your journey of REI.

◊ Get Schooled

Sometimes, another barrier to getting started is knowledge about the industry and the investing process. Although there is a great deal to learn, it can be accomplished in small portions as you work through the development of your real estate investing plan.

Just as with the medical and legal professions, or even the discipline of an engineer, each has their technical verbiage. The real estate industry is no different. What is different with REI, is that learning and understanding the lingo, the definitions, and the formulas, is relatively easy to comprehend as you go through each step of the process.

◊ Don't Bet on Perfection

Real estate investing is a business. To create a new business, sometimes individuals want to put all the pieces in place and get it perfect before getting started.

It is helpful to remember that the perfect plan does not and cannot exist because we are imperfect human beings, and therefore, lack the ability to create anything perfect. It is best to keep the planning and process very simple.

◊ Establish Resource Pools

Although it is not my intent to promote any particular resource pools, I will mention a few that are commonly in use. You, however, will be able to expand your resource pool as you progress through the process.

The Internet has an abundance of free information, much of which can be validated to help you in getting started. One of my daughters refers to Google as her business partner. She uses it as a tool to research and verify almost everything she does.

I have another acquaintance who suggests if you cannot find instructions on how to repair an item or complete a particular task or process using the YouTube website, the solution does not exist.

Another resource could be the local libraries or investing groups. You can further realize benefits by connecting with other like-minded individuals to learn as well as share information and experiences to meet your needs—and therein, establish a support network for your business.

What Being a REI Can Do For You

You may have various reasons for becoming a real estate investor. You may what to:

- Build your nest egg
- Live your dreams
- Feed your family
- Buy that yacht
- Give yourself a steady income
- Give yourself peace of mind
- Change your life

To add to the list of reasons above, take the next step and leap to create something bigger than yourself. Determine what your profitability would mean, well beyond your personal and family goals. With the money you make, with the skills you acquire—along with property—consider how could you change someone's life!

◊ See Your Vision

So, yes. I want to ensure that my family is being cared for both now and long after I'm gone. It is my dream to leave them a legacy they cannot only be proud of, but one where meeting their future needs will always exist.

However, far beyond my personal needs and objectives, I have a bigger vision. I want to empower minorities and help disenfranchised communities and neighborhoods to rebuild and reinvest in themselves. All by teaching individuals, like you, how to envision and achieve a higher quality of life and opportunity through real estate investing.

◊ Create Your Mission

Asked during a real estate investing symposium what my goal and my mission are, I shared my thoughts to see if they might have been in alignment with the presenters' ideas. However, as I spoke of my mission, one person wasn't so sure about how realistic I was.

Well, it has been my experience that if you can write down your goal, dream, vision, and mission—and you direct your focus—you can achieve it.

So what is my mission? To be in line with my vision, I will empower one hundred people in my immediate circle within the next year to become millionaires based on their asset value. You are one of my hundred.

Once you hit the first million the rest of it is easy, creating a snowball effect. You know the process; you have the knowledge now to have ten or fifteen million dollars in assets. You will be able to work with the kids in the community to encourage them to envision, and to motivate them to a point where they feel empowered, as if nothing could stop them from doing, being, or having whatever they dream. That, to me, would be a great gift.

◊ Anybody Can Do Investing

When I said anybody could do real estate investing, I believe anybody can do it if they want to. As with anything in life, if your heart isn't in the game, if you can't get excited about what you are doing, can't find any enjoyment, or some pleasure in your work, then you should move on to something else. Because if you stay in, especially, if all you want to do is make a buck or two, you'll be doing your clients a great disservice. Also, and you may already know this, your health and that of those around you may suffer, as well.

◊ Investing is a Challenge

Real estate investing is taking on a situation tor a challenge that gives you a glimmer of the potential but does not offer a clear view of what the outcome will be.

Controlling costs with an acquisition can be challenging. There are repair bills, tax bills, and zoning permits to consider.

Finding someone that likes what you develop or what you created and who is willing to buy the property from you at the profit you seek can also be a challenge.

By crafting and developing the real estate investment plan for each property in which you invest, your anticipated outcome and profit become more likely what you want them to be. It's this process that allows you to take and change a situation or an object from nothing, and perhaps, sight unseen, into something that is not only profitable for you, but beneficial to the other party involved and, possibly, even the broader community.

Summary

And so, One of My Hundred, this begins your training to become the best, and most successful Real Estate Investor you've envisioned becoming.

Notes & Review

This section is for your use to make note of any ideas that came to you while reading the chapter.

This section will also contain 3-5 questions that were asked within the chapter. Space has been provided for you to record your answers.

1. What brought you to this book and what questions did you have that you hoped to find the answers?

_____

_____

_____

_____

_____

_____

_____

2. What is your vision?

_____

_____

_____

_____

_____

3. What is your mission?

_____

_____

_____

_____

_____

_____

Additional Notes

_____

_____

_____

_____

_____

~ 2 ~

The Big Why

In the first chapter, you learned about the world of real estate investing. It can be a very lucrative business endeavor whether practiced full-time or part-time.

People get into the business for many reasons. Some love the thrill of the chase. A few may be following a parent's footsteps. Others may see a bigger picture to help a community rebuild.

Going into any business or career is a decision to be made with eyes wide open and forethought. However, as in any field of choice, there is the good, the bad, and the ugly.

Let's look at each and their outcomes.

The Ugly

The ugly does not necessarily pertain to the property, although, it could. Primarily it relates to the results from poor or unwise decisions arising from inaccurate information, most likely from uninformed advisers, lack of personal knowledge or resources not specifically suited to your needs for your investment objectives.

The Bad

The bad comes in many forms and on many levels, and generally when the information you received is inadequate or inaccurate. When the foundation of your real estate investment decisions is flawed, it is very likely your investment choices will not provide the important outcomes you anticipate and desire.

Bad is obviously not good. It creates discomfort, losses, distaste, and dissatisfied partners—including your lender or other people on whom you rely.

Without the persistence required by a successful real estate investor, bad investment choices could be a great discouragement to the average person and create enough frustration to seek out another career.

◊ Lost the Lust

Someone I know had decided to pursue real estate investments no longer. He had lost the hunger for the business. As I look back on his career, he started many years ago and on the wrong track. He thought the process was just a matter of talking to someone about a property, creating a contract, and then getting a contractor to do the repairs. Ba-da-bing-ba-da-boom. Deal completed. No wonder his passion was gone. There was no chase, no excitement, and no drive or motivation to keep him going.

◊ Long Hours

A new investor will work long hours. As with any new job, there is training involved. To properly learn the ins and outs of investing you may need to put in 30 to 90 days of education in addition to the hands-on experience while in the trenches.

Unlike my friend who lost his passion, you must be willing to go the distance and get several quotes and estimates on repairs for a single acquisition. And all this takes time and patience.

◊ Risky Business

There are inherent risks of which any new or even seasoned investors need to be aware. Real estate investing can get a bad name quickly, and so can the investor. If not properly educated in the schoolroom or the field, you won't be effective, make profits, or be the success of which you once dreamed. Work habits, once developed, are not easily or simply turned around.

As my friend found, working off of one estimate (that may have been from another friend) may not be an accurate representation of what the property is worth or how much repairs will be. Two months later while negotiations may still be happening, money is lost and so is the deal, and probably given to another investor.

There is risk everywhere in life. However, when you start the business on the right foot, with the tools and knowledge received by getting trained and coached, you can do real estate investing—and keep the passion alive; so much so that failure will not be an option.

The Good & Upside of Becoming a REI

To gain a clearer picture, let's review the role of a real estate investor. A real estate investor is simply an individual who buys and then sells the property for profit—the process is done either directly or indirectly. It could involve the renovation or improvement of the asset before being sold.

An investor directly participating in the business of buying and selling is called an active real estate investor. An individual or entity using a real estate investment trust, syndicates, or other investment vehicles, in which they have no direct participation or management—but where they place funds to profit from real estate holdings or transactions—refers to a passive real estate investor.

The idea behind this business of investing—and this book—is to acquire property that is in need of repair, fix it up, and then dispose of the asset for more money than you put into it, and repeat the process as often as necessary to reach your financial goal.

Part of your investment strategies might dictate acquiring rental income property as part of your real estate investment portfolio. This action would necessitate buying property at such a price point which would allow for its acquisition, improvements, and maintenance costs to yield a reasonable profit on your investment, and one consistent with the benchmark you anticipate for a return.

In other words, your total rent from the investment property would have to cover its monthly operating expenses, such as taxes and insurance. You would also have to cover the carrying cost, which is the monthly mortgage payment inclusive of principal and interest—and in addition to the profit—you anticipate from the asset each month.

Some transactions are expected to yield immediate returns. Other deals may be intended for equity development over time. The strategy for each acquisition may be different.

If you are excited about the prospect of making a lot of money, yet, still uncertain this is the road you should be on, maybe the following reasons will help with your decision.

◊ Make Big Money Fast

The idea behind investing in real estate is to generate revenue so that you have money to either spend on your life desires, such as travel, paying your child or grandkid's college expenses, save for your retirement, or take that excess build-up and reinvest into more property assets. The dollars that accumulate over time from a positive cash flow can change lives—and not just yours.

◊ World-Wide Reach

There are many different types of real estate property from which you can select for your investing business. The range varies from condemned property all the way up to luxury properties.

Would you like to travel? When investing in property, you are open to anywhere in the world. A word of caution, though, first: stay local and in your backyard until you become seasoned and profitable, and then you are free to move about the world.

◊ Change Communities for the Better

A personal reason of mine in becoming a real estate investor is to help struggling communities rebuild. To affect real change, one must begin by finding individuals with the same values, because, and although you would like to think so, you cannot be in or do this business alone. It is my goal to find people like you to teach, coach, and mentor who want to become real estate investors to bring wealth back into their communities so they can once again thrive.

Gaining Confidence Over Fear

You may worry about personal sustainability with regards to your finances and health. So, you take actionable steps, such as getting a job or becoming a real estate investor, to thwart adverse circumstances.

Fear can be the reason you do something or do nothing. You may be fearful of losing a significant benefit from an action, or you may be too afraid to take action. Neither of which is any good.

The real estate investing business is vast. And because of that larger than life existence, getting into the game of REI can be scary. Often, if afraid, panic settles in, and that is the time when mistakes can occur.

So how do you go from being afraid at every step to being confident?

◊ Get Schooled

Knowledge and confidence are tied closely together. Gaining proficiency in whatever you do will obliterate any fear. In the world of REI, you must learn about market values and how to do property analysis. To make the wise and right decision about an asset, understanding how to accomplish those items can be a key to your success. When you buy at the right price and allowing for contingencies (cost items not immediately seen, but could arise in the future), your profits can become more reliable from the accurate calculation on your part.

◊ Practice

You also gain knowledge by practical application. When working with somebody who has experience—and perhaps, has made unwise decisions that cost them a lot of money—can catch you at the moment before you go down a wrong path.

It is important to concentrate on one area only of investing until you become proficient—whether it is single family or small multi-family homes. The more you practice within one focused sector, the more knowledgeable you become with the process, players, and your options.

Also with practice, you begin to know the competition within your marketplace and can anticipate their moves. The more knowledge you possess of the resources involved, the easier to compete and win.

◊ Build Foundation

As in any business, and especially if you want to be a real estate investor you cannot start without some foundation. For instance, you have to understand a few principles of the real estate industry and its market. You also should have knowledge about the investing process, and how money (both surplus and lack) effects your ability to function in the real estate investor arena. Additionally, you should develop a network of buyers and sellers and financial resources.

Having the right people, knowledge, and resources to help you make good decisions with your investments will increase your confidence level, which is an essential piece for both the investor and the process. Plus, the confidence in your decision comes from knowing what you're going to do and how you're going to do it before getting started.

Is Investing Really For Me?

You've already heard me say that I believe anybody can be a real estate investor if they want to. However, and once again, with anything in life, if your heart is not there, if you can't get excited about what you do, if some enjoyment, some pleasure in the work is not present, I don't think you should do it, period. There are two reasons as mentioned earlier in this chapter: a disservice and a health hazard to you and those with whom you work.

If you have a passion for helping people realize their dreams, if you love a career that contains a good challenge, exciting opportunities, and carries a small potential to make you lots of money, then real estate investing just may be your ticket to a financially successful career.

And you've also heard me say being a real estate investor means taking on a situation when you don't know what the outcome will be. By crafting and developing a plan, creating a track to take a property that's like a diamond in the rough, turn it into a polished work of art, and yielding a decent profit you will have successfully overcome the challenges. You have created something out of nothing. The process and the feeling of accomplishment are quite rewarding.

Why Not Just Become a Real Estate Agent?

One of the differences between an investor and an agent is licensing. A real estate agent must be licensed and then find a broker with whom to work. The real estate investor has autonomy to go where the deals are, but not required to be licensed.

Another difference is commission based (the agent) versus profit realized (the investor).

On the one hand, should you decide first to become an agent, you will gain more knowledge about the real estate market surely, and you could also save a bit of money in not having to pay commission to anyone for finding the property; however, I consider that a bit short-sighted.

On the other hand, should you decide to be your own agent, you will have less time to pay attention to other details of the business. With the extra time you have by not playing the role of an agent you can check up on the contractor work on the other investments. Plus with the extra time you can seek additional property in which to invest.

Also, and as an investor, essentially what you do is contribute to your local economy by engaging real estate agents to help find your property. You bring in the flow of money not only to your locality but also to the agent who is passionate about the service they give to their community.

To realize the maximum value of return for any time spent on a specific activity, you must, as an entrepreneurial investor, determine the highest and best use of your time.

For example, consider the value of a real estate agent's research to be $100 an hour. You, as the investor, did the same work, but the value to your business is at a modest $500 an hour. With the $400 difference, would it not be in your best interest to allow the real estate agent to assist you?

The time and money you save can be put toward either another opportunity or quality family outings.

Summary

There are many certain and exciting reasons as to the why of becoming a real estate investor. If you can agree to at least three of them listed below—and you may have a few of your own—then this career just might be for you.

I am interested in becoming a real estate investor because I want to:
- Make more money
- Support my family
- Have more time with my family
- Help other people succeed
- Put people to work
- Put more funds into my community

- Have safe neighborhoods
- Build up run-down communities
- Have fun in what I do
- I want to share my passion with others

Notes & Review

This section is for your use to make note of any ideas that came to you while reading the chapter.

This section will also allow space for you to record the answer to the all important question of why you want to become a real estate investor.

1. List below any reasons you can think of for wanting this option for a career.

_____

_____

_____

_____

_____

_____

_____

_____

_____

Additional Notes

_____

_____

_____

_____

_____

_____

_____

_____

_____

_____

_____

~ 3 ~

The Set-Up

Real estate is a source you can use to generate cash. It is highly recommended to buy and sell assets to accumulate enough money so you can make future investment decisions comfortably—sans stress and emotion—and without adding to the expenses by paying loan interest to an outside resource or financier. Keep in mind that what is comfortable for one person may not be comfortable to another.

For instance, I believe having a half-million dollars in liquidity is a good place to start when you are buying and selling or buying and holding property. Somewhere between three and five hundred thousand will give you that comfort level. Two hundred thousand dollars allows you to look at the property, but with more liquidity in your pocket, however, you will have the resources at the ready. You may also worry less if a situation arises that requires more of your investment money.

Good Rules of Thumb for New Investors

However, first things first. There are a few pieces that must be put into place before you begin building the puzzle.

◊ Get Seasoned & Knowledgeable

Start with the basics and simple projects. When working in the rehab market of real estate, there are many choices, such as properties that need easy-to-do kitchen or bathroom renovations. By moving through one or two of these, and setting aside a bit of the profit on a regular basis, you can then expand your operational program to include larger projects.

Confidence comes from the practical knowledge.

◊ Form LLC

In most states, anything to do with real estate must be in writing. Forming a Limited Liability Corporation (LLC) or other organization is highly recommended and carries self-protection value as far as your personal assets are concerned. Organizing your business is one of the best and wisest decisions you will make in your real estate investing career.

◊ Stay Local

It is best to start investing in an area with which you are familiar, or can become familiar, relatively quickly. A good rule of thumb is to consider working within a circumference of one or two hours of the area in which you reside. Once you have mastered the art of investing locally you can certainly journey into new markets.

◊ Secure a Reserve of Funds

It is entirely possible to fund deals without much, or any, of your capital. You don't need tens of thousands of dollars, but you should have some money to be able to start marketing.

Little things like business cards, investment club fees, updated phones or computers and cash set aside for marketing purposes are helpful.

There are many free websites, such as Craigslist, and internet resources, such as email campaign software, that are available to get you started. You can also reach out to friends and family to see if they have any interest in either funding deals or know someone who is currently interested in selling an asset.

Even if it is a few thousand dollars, you should have some reserves to begin marketing when first starting out.

◊ Know Your Strategy Before Investing

The ultimate goal you want to achieve remains generating enough revenue so you can make real estate investing decisions in a comfortable or no-stress situation.

Up to this point, you have been thinking through the process. Now it is time to develop a sound real estate investing plan and the strategy to support it.

◊ Have a Firm Plan

With so much at stake in regards to time, money, and energy, you don't want to make up the process as you go. To eliminate the guesswork as much as possible while moving through a real estate investing transaction, a solid plan in place will ensure your success. Although I mentioned that you don't need an office, a website, business cards, or the approval of your best friend or family member to begin, you do need a plan.

Listed below are a few questions that should be asked of yourself.

- What is your initial investing strategy for your real estate business?
- How are you going to finance deals that come your way?
- In what markets and specific areas are you looking?

It is best to perfect your skills and master a market in one area before attempting any expansion. Trying different directions, initially, could impede your progress and be very costly in two things you cannot afford to squander—time and money.

You don't need to know every step you will take on every deal, but you do need to have a clear vision for what your real estate goals are. These goals will help you to choose the best team and on which properties you will make offers. Instead of worrying about the minutia of the business, start by developing a plan for how you want to get there.

◊ Build a Solid, Collaborative Network Team

Real estate is a people business. As a smart investor, you would want to have key professionals as partners who have in-depth knowledge of each aspect in the real estate investing process.

Every transaction requires a working rapport with several individuals for a project to go smoothly, and so working with a good team is in your best interest.

Finding this team before your first deal is not as challenging as it may appear. If you know what you want, a good team can help you make it happen.

The clearer you are with your plan, the easier it will be for them to do their job.

Lawyer

A knowledgeable real estate attorney with expertise in the markets where you are investing is a valuable asset to your team. An attorney will provide legal advice, directions, documentations, and review on several legal matters.

A well-versed attorney will be able to monitor, manage, and provide the legal framework in which to function to keep the project legitimate and profitable. He or she would also be able to discern and disseminate clear titles and deeds.

Accountant

Good money management is a necessity to ensure the funds are properly tracked and dispersed. There is a level of discipline required that you may not have where money is concerned. Therefore, obtaining an accountant who has a strong background in real estate is of the essence, and especially, to ensure the funds are doled out for their intended use.

For instance, you, as an investor, have set aside money for a project. However, an emergency comes up, such as a death or serious illness in the family. The temptation may be—if you cannot manage money well or do not have the discipline to keep the funds where they are— that you use the available funds for the immediate problem, which could devastate both the current project and future investments.

Regardless that you are good at managing money, an experienced accountant possesses the knowledge, skill, and perhaps, more importantly, the discipline necessary to ensure the success of the overall transaction. An accountant can act as a good fiscal adviser and may also be able to use your financial resources to leverage funds from other clients who may have similar interests.

Contractors

If your strategy is to focus on rehabs (the primary focus of this book), you need the help of a reliable contractor. They will have a direct impact on the quality of work and, whether or not, you stay under budget.

Competent and reliable contractors can provide estimates of repairs needed on the property. These contractors will also come in handy to confirm the substance of the property inspection report. Contractors can include building inspectors, roofers, pest control, plumbers, and electricians.

Be sure to have four or five contractors for each discipline. When going over property, to get a good sense of its condition, it is recommended to complete three sets of evaluations. And so, having lots of contractors in your back pocket will ensure, as much as possible, that there will be no unwanted surprises once renovations begin.

Mortgage Brokers & Lenders

Mortgage brokers work with multiple lending institutions. A loan originator usually collaborates with a particular agency. A mortgage broker can represent multiple institutions conventional or private, and a commercial loan broker facilitates private transactions relative to individuals or entities utilizing private (or hard money) for their purchases.

These transactions are typically not subject to RESPA, the Real Estate Settlement Procedures Act.

You will also need a good mortgage broker or lender to finance your deals. For what you want to do may not be in line with what is approved. A good lender knows the best programs for you and can get your deals done as quickly as possible. You can also use private money lenders by building relationships with people looking to lend.

Credit can sometimes be a concern depending on the type of lender from which you intend to seek funds. However, it does not have to be a barrier to your real estate investment success because of the many alternatives that are available. Options can include partnering with someone with good credit to qualify for a specific loan or line of credit. They may also include the use of loans not based on credit, although the cost of those loans may be higher. Resources may also be available through real estate investing coaches and the relationships they have developed.

Real Estate Agent

To incorporate the help of a real estate agent may seem odd, but you do want someone who is familiar with the area, the territory of where you are looking to invest. You also want to find an agent who is investor-friendly. It is recommended to have a few agents at your disposal. For it is the real estate agent who will be able to identify the properties in which you are specifically interested and can match your goals.

Plus, by employing an agent, your time will be spent more wisely on investing activities versus having to locate the assets, too. The agent will also be able to assess the property's value as is and after any repairs are complete. You can then make an informed decision as to whether or not the acquisition is right for you. The agent can also assist with market analysis, property values, and buyers who may be ready to acquire your redeveloped properties.

How many properties are you looking to purchase this year? Can you take on a full renovation, sometimes referred to as a "full gut?" What about adding an addition, or are you just looking for properties that need cosmetic work? These questions will best help a real estate agent that is working for you and your business.

◊ Hire a Real Estate Investment Coach

If you're just starting out you don't want to go down this road alone, nor do you want to reinvent the wheel. Walk with somebody who has done this before and also to get those questions answered.

You may have heard that you don't need to be smart to be successful, you just have to have a lot of smart people around you. It is true!

I had a great mentoring coach, and to this day I have several mentors that I call upon to help me with different situations. A few of them require a bit of an investment, but you can expect that in the real estate world. Without their advice, I would not have gotten through certain situations as well as I had.

So the bottom line, as a real estate investor, not only do you need coaching, you also need to know what to do, when to do it, but also how to do it, too. That is not something you pick up by osmosis.

And if you try working through the process even after an intensive real estate training program at a college or other type of school you still have to practice—as in the real world of practice, which is very different to the academic process. The practical application provides an experience which you need to develop to be successful in real estate investing.

◊ Secure Additional Resources

In addition to needing somebody to guide you through the practical process a number of times, and I emphasize a number of times, you also need experienced investment practitioners to guide you through the complexity of and pieces associated with a transaction. These types of resources, however, are at a premium—meaning they are not free just for the asking or because you are a nice person.

If you're going to make money with somebody's knowledge and experience it ought to be understood, or reasonable, that you are willing to compensate the experienced person for their knowledge. If you are a bit pressed for cash, an arrangement could be suggested, such as you would be willing to share the resources that you develop as a part of that process.

There are too many things that you need to know intricately and intimately on what to do to end the transaction with the most profit possible.

Entering into the investing arena without a coach or mentor could cost you in the long-run. Oh sure, you can do a real estate transaction. However, if you want to gain the most profit from a sale you need to invest in the resources.

◊ Research the Field of Real Estate

Before finding property, you must be aware of the type you are seeking. Are you looking for wholesale Tier 1, direct business with banks or other institutional activity? Or are you looking at Tier 2, other individual investors or persons who may be selling single properties or small bundles, such as 1 to 10 properties or more at a time?

Are you looking for distressed properties or opportunities through short sales, pre-foreclosures, probate (divorce or death)? How about fire damaged or flooded properties?

Perhaps you would like to help the elderly who seek to move from independent living into a group living arrangement, and no longer want the responsibility of home ownership? Some homeowners, of whom as a result of their age, are not interested or motivated by lots of money, but are more interested in supporting a cause.

What is your cause? How are you going to fund or finance real estate opportunities you identify?

19 Real Estate Investing Opportunities

Below is a list of 19 different investing opportunities available to you. There are many more, but choosing one or two will give a good beginning at your career.

- Abandoned properties
- Absentee property owners
- Condemned properties
- Development in default
- Distressed property institutions
- Distressed property owners individuals
- Elderly acquisition
- Estate sales
- Foreclosed properties
- Lawful property seizures
- Probate debt, divorce
- Properties at risk for delinquent taxes or other liens
- Properties damaged by fire or natural disaster
- Properties developed and leased up for cash flow purposes
- Properties discounted quick disposition relative to flight for safety
- Properties in receivership
- Property sold at auction
- Short sale
- Underutilized commercial properties

◊ Complete an Analysis

Your fundamental responsibility is to become familiar with the areas of interest and the agencies and vendors in which you will work. You will also need to identify your specific real estate market, the type of property, and the amount of time, on average, it takes to sell a property. Note that the quicker a property sells, generally, the more desirable the market is to investors.

The most important part of the investment process is having buyers ready to purchase the properties after your acquisition. As you practice with each transaction, you will develop the sense of timing.

During the investment process I suggest you:
1. Precisely determine what your target asset will be.
2. Scan the market availability and determine the maximum that you are willing to pay for a property.
3. Considering its condition, adjust your offer price consistent with any repairs or upgrades that may be necessary to become comparable with other properties in the neighborhood.

As an investor, please note your acquisitions should be at the wholesale level, to allow retail disposition with the margins on which you plan or intend.

◊ Finance Options

Even though that accumulated cash, which remains king, puts you into a powerful state of play, it is a good idea to have other financial resources available. You never know what you'll run into while going through the acquisition disposition process. Those outside sources may provide a cushion, a type of comfort zone that you can tap into in the event additional money is needed because of unforeseen circumstances.

◊ Be Purpose-Driven

As much as you would like to believe, deals will not just fall into your lap. New investors, in particular, will find this to be even truer.

Real estate is not an "easy" business, but it certainly can be fun and very competitive. It takes tenacity, persistence, discipline, and the will to succeed no matter what. Regardless of how experienced you are, deals take work—which may mean stepping out of your comfort zone and calling 100 new contacts a day. It could mean knocking on every door just to get one new lead. Most new deals typically go to the person who has the most drive and works the hardest to get them. When you are just getting going, it can be the most frustrating time in the business. There will be days where you are working hard, but not seeing anything for it.

The successful investors are those that fight through those days and commit to work even harder. If you have only one attribute, you must have the drive to succeed. In time, and with the right mindset, everything else will eventually fall into place. Without drive and determination, nothing else matters.

Not everything is going to be perfect in your first couple of months. However, this doesn't mean you shouldn't get started. Every investor in a meeting has been in the same position you are. Those that have been in business for some time managed to get to where they are by being persistent and fighting through the tough days. The longer you wait to get started, the more difficult it becomes.

Summary

The process of real estate investing may seem large and daunting to accomplish. But when you have a plan in place and follow it, you are rewarded for your effort.

Below is a recap of what's necessary for the process.

- Get Seasoned and Knowledgeable
- Form LLC
- Stay Local
- Secure a Reserve of Funds
- Know Your Strategy Before Investing
- Create a Firm Plan
- Build a Solid Team and Collaborative Network
- Hire Coaches and Additional Resources
- Research the Field of Real Estate Opportunities
- Be Purpose-Driven

Notes & Review

This section is for your use to make note of any ideas that came to you while reading the chapter.

This section will also contain questions that were asked within the chapter. Space has been provided for you to record your answers.

1. What is your initial investing strategy for your real estate business?

_____

_____

_____

_____

2. How are you going to finance deals that come your way?

_____

_____

_____

_____

3. In what markets and specific areas are you looking?

_____

_____

_____

4. What type of property will you be looking for?

_____

_____

_____

Additional Notes

_____

_____

_____

_____

_____

_____

~ 4 ~

The Market

Imagine being a new real estate investor and not knowing anything about the markets in which you hope to invest. It only makes sense that determining the particular real estate market would be the next step after choosing the career of an investor.

From Land to Sea

The real estate market runs from everything you see on the piece of land to the sea that abuts it. Plus, there are sub-markets within each major market of the real estate realm. One must pay attention to economic and financial markets, locales, construction markets, any area which impacts the buying and selling process.

◊ Residential Market

Single-family homes, two-family homes, such as a condominium or townhouse, and, of course, the luxury homes make up the residential market.

Most investors who are first entering into real estate explore the residential field as a path into the bigger real estate investment arena. Also, seasoned real estate investors recommend beginning in this market. Once you have the experience, know the process, and have cash built up, then you can move on to pursue other available markets.

◊ Commercial Market

You may think of storefront buildings, businesses, shopping centers, or strip malls when you hear of the commercial market. However, the commercial market can also expand on the residential with four- or eight-unit buildings. These are considered to be multi-family-small units. Apartment buildings where, for example, 200 families live are deemed to be multi-family-large units.

Working in commercial real estate has a steep learning curve and can take lots of time to absorb and make wise decisions with regards to investing.

◊ Other Markets

In chapter 3 you learned of 19 real estate property opportunities from which to choose for your investment. You could say that those opportunities are mini-markets within the entire, overall housing market. Each one of those opportunities can happen in any one of the major markets—agricultural, industrial, medical, or government, just to name a few. While they are worthwhile, it is beyond the scope of this book to touch on each one in depth, other than when making a point of comparison.

◊ Dollar Range of Markets

In today's market, different investors choose different spheres in the marketplace when it comes to the amount of dollars they wish to use for investing.

- Low: $0–$300,000
- Medium: $301,000–$699,999
- High: $700,000–$999,999
- Luxury: $1,000,000 and above

Most people can buy the low to low-medium range simply based on resource limitations or regarding the speed of turnover in the marketplace. And of course, high to luxury market priced homes are at the top of the pinnacle. Many prefer the middle market because of the demand in that area.

Private funders/lenders are serving all levels of investments. Several lenders reason that it takes the same amount of time to make a small loan as it does to make a mid-size loan but they make a lot less money. Therefore, although they may be the most affordable to do, those projects may be a bit harder to get funded or may require a larger contribution from you to make the transaction work.

It is important for you to consider which market according to dollar range you desire to enter. If you are starting with no knowledge, I suggest beginning with the lower end of the dollar range until you gain some smarts and cash in your pocket.

◊ Location, Location, Location

In real estate, there is the saying that location is everything. This adage is true and should be something to consider when looking at property for investment purposes. Although it may not seem so, location is a key concern and one that speaks to markets as well.

Whether you are in California, Kansas, or Massachusetts, your income is going to determine how much you can buy. For instance, if you live in the Boston area, compared to other large cities across the United States, the housing costs are higher. So, if you stick to that $300,000 or less range, there's going to be fewer properties from which to choose.

Local

You may hear this next concept over and over again, but I believe it is important for an investor to become seasoned and knowledgeable with some experience before they do anything outside of their immediate area.

If you set your sight on property well within driving distance, say 40 or 60 miles, you will be able to efficiently manage the needs of the process if you must get to the site quickly.

Don't worry. You will find plenty of options within a one-hour radius of your home base, especially if you live in an urban area. If you live in a suburban or remote (rural) area you might have to increase the time a bit. You want to be within reach of the property to oversee, touch, and feel what is happening during the buying, selling, and investment process.

Out-of-State

In a few states where properties are valued and priced lower, such as Alabama or Missouri, there is more opportunity for investing rather than states such as New York or Virginia and may be of interest to you.

In some cases you may want to work with a family member in an out-of-state situation. The following is my cautionary tale of working with a family member in a long-distance partnership.

I, at one time, bought five properties in Virginia for a relative to redevelop. Although able to fund the entire project emergencies came up for me where I had to dip into the cash reserve. Plus, the relative had a few challenges afterward, too. All those funds ended up going somewhere else other than where originally dedicated. I wound up in a big hole, losing a lot of money, and the properties never got redeveloped.

The above story also shows why it is recommended to stay within an hour's travel from your home. With my being in Boston and managing the investment process in another state—and on several properties at the same time—I was not able to keep a good enough watch.

I share this warning with you in hopes you don't make the same mistake.

However, if you are sure your plans include an out-of-state location be certain to collaborate with somebody—and especially not with a relative—who does know that part of the town, city, county, or state.

International

The same advice given in the out-of-state section above goes for the global real estate market investing process. Get knowledgeable and with a trusted and established partner before entering into any foreign market.

◊ Trash or Treasure?

Different people see things different ways. One investor may see a community that has, and is known for lots of violence, as dangerous, and not want to do any investing there.

Another investor will look at the same community and say, "You know, at some point in time that violence has to stop. Right now is an excellent opportunity to buy. And if the price is right my profits may be bigger."

Each investor has their idea of what a property could and would not do for them. It's personal as well as business. Some are community-oriented and can see—visualize—the communities bounce back in such a way that makes their investment worthwhile.

While other investors who are driven solely by money and profit may not look at that community the same way and see their investment dwindling or as a waste of time and energy.

Trash or treasure? It's a matter of taste and interest and ambition.

Beauty & Dollars in the Eye of the Beholder

There is something said for those who can take the oldest and most disheveled piece of property and see the inner beauty, the dollars for which it could bring.

For example, I know of an area where many of the three-family homes would typically sell for, in this current market, around $500,000 to $600,000. An investor with vision who came to play might take that multi-family housing, split the apartments into single family condominium units, and then sell them for roughly $300,000 each.

Because of that vision, that same property has a $900,000 return on sale, a three to four hundred thousand dollar profit higher than the standard $500,000 received as one solid unit.

Of course, there is more to this process in particular described throughout this book. Imagine what can be done with collaboration while working with a coach or mentor who has this kind of vision. More about this later.

Some of the other factors investors look at while seeking property are the following:

- State of the neighborhood
- The amount of criminal activity
- Businesses within the area
- Type of community

The decision is total individual investor preference.

◊ Consider Hold Time with Buying and Selling

Some investors are looking for properties to buy and hold, and some investors are constantly in the buy-sell mode. The type of investment determines what happens to the property.

During your consideration phase, take into account that all markets will not be at the same level at the same time. Also, while viewing the marketplace, you may want to consider how you will go about the transaction. For instance, are you looking at the deal as quick, such as to fix up and sell, or will you hold onto the property and use it for rental revenue? And if either of these is a consideration, how long will the property stay in your asset portfolio?

And much, of course, depends on the price of the property and what you propose to do with it. If it's an asset that will provide high returns, the investor may decide to keep it for rental. The profit in the property interestingly enough is anticipated or seen when you buy the property, not when you sell.

In anticipation of a certain profit, buying property at the right price is essential to the timing of how long you hang on to it.

30-60-90 Day Turnarounds

In most markets investors will go after property in areas they know will sell in four months; these are usually single family homes. Being tied to property any longer than that, the investor will want to ensure cash flow—typically received from existing rental units—and is adequate to cover the costs until a fruitful and profitable sale.

120 Days or more

If buying property at the top of your investment strategy and you find your cash position is absolute, that you can carry both the property and its current cash flow, you may want to keep it until you wish to sell. The choice is yours. However, you must do your homework before the investment.

An Example

Let's say you acquire a three-family property for $100,000. The place was not kept up due to the health of the owner, who has now died. The property needs a lot of repairs because pigeons live on the roof. You put an additional $200,000 into the three-family unit to fix it up. You are now in $300,000 for that property. After the repairs are complete, you can sell the property for $400,000 at a $100,000 profit.

You could instead, and depending on location, collect $2,000 a month per unit in rent. Therefore, with the rental income from this property yielding $72,000 a year, you will be able to recover your investment in just a little over four years.

What you decide to do with the property, whether to keep or dispose of it, is your choice, and again, one before you invest.

◊ Take Time to Learn the Ropes

Real estate investing is not a quick get-rich scheme. As a beginner investor, it is wise to take the time to build as you learn and understand how the market works. It would be inadvisable, not to mention a bit foolish, to rush in to make a purchase just to create a fast buck or two, even if you think you know the area or believe you comprehend the process.

Your investment opportunity has to be the right purchase to make you the profit which you seek—and those don't come up every day.

Slow and Steady Wins the Race

Do your due diligence. Be patient and wait for the right opportunity—this cannot be emphasized enough. Think of the process as a horse race. There are ten races on which you can place a bet. Now, another peer investor bets on every race without any forethought, hoping to win big.

You, on the other hand, go to the racetrack with a strategy. You researched each horse that is racing during the day, comparing the animals with similar backgrounds that previously won races. You carefully select two horses with the expectation one of those horses will give you the return on your five- or ten-dollar investment. I am by no means herein advocating gambling. Knowledge and a plan with efficient execution are the keys to increasing the probability of your success.

Who will go home a happy camper? Chances are the investor who did his or her homework.

Pay Attention to the Economic Market

Remember reading about how there are markets within markets? Following the economic market is an important part of being an investor. You must know what is happening with the almighty dollar in the area where you wish to work. If there is a downturn or the stock market declines without bouncing back, you may need to research areas where the economy may not play a significant role to avoid the risk of financial loss.

Mitigate Risk

Even with a lot of opportunities, however, there is risk associated with them all. Having the patience to wait for the right situation to come along may be a big challenge for you, as a beginning investor. You are excited to start. You are ready to make money.

Often, if you get off on the wrong foot, or are led down a wrong path by not having the right guidance, a bad decision could be made that takes you out of the game for good.

Reading this book will help mitigate some of the risks as you will have a foundation of knowledge and understanding before you go out on your own. Hiring a coach or mentor will further mitigate the risk of bad investments.

◊ Study the MLS

There are best practices to follow to improve your chances of success as a real estate investor.

Get an Expert

The inclination as an investor would be to look at the MLS (Multiple Listing Service). However, as a new investor, do you know how to read the information contained in the report? You may figure it out over time, yet, how much time are you willing to spend in ramping up that knowledge? By working with someone experienced to help you process the content would get you up to speed in no time.

So, the first step in learning the market is to get someone on your team that is knowledgeable, preferably an expert that can help you wade through the information.

Discern the Available Property

You do need to know what property is available, where you can go after it, and how long it has been on the market. The MLS is a great place to find that information.

Often in the MLS, however, the property has been listed for a short amount time, 30 days or less, for example, which may not be in your best interests to pursue. The property may not be able to turn the profit for which you hope.

The 90-Day Listings

Chances are items that are on the MLS for 90 days, or more, have something wrong with the property itself or its location. The condition of the building is not up to code; the location is not what it should be, or something entirely different.

As you complete research on these properties, especially if you are interested in it, you must ask the question, "What is it about this property that has kept it on the market for 90 days?"

If you find that the property is in good condition, then move on to the next probable cause—location. Look at the police blotter for that area. Is there a high rate of crime? Are there environmental issues, such as is there a nuclear energy plant nearby?

If you are serious about acquiring one of these properties, then look for a buyer that is hungry and willing to live anywhere, just to have a place to call home.

Does this marketing practice seem a bit crude? Maybe. Consider the person that doesn't care about where they live, they just want someplace to call their own. If the price is right regardless of location, somebody will buy the property.

A good point to remember is that your profit is made when you purchase the property not when you sell it. It is essential that you buy at the right price to repair when necessary and sell to obtain your anticipated margin of profit.

Summary

Below is a recap of what's needed before you randomly select a property in which to invest.

- Explore your options within the real estate market
- Decide on the location of where you want to begin
- Make a plan before you buy, deciding whether or not to keep the property
- Estimate the length of time to hold or release
- Take time to learn the market
- Become familiar with the MLS

Notes & Review

This section is for your use to make note of any ideas that came to you while reading the chapter.

This section will also contain questions that were asked within the chapter. Space has been provided for you to record your answers.

1. Will you buy and sell or hold property? Why or why not?

_____

_____

_____

_____

_____

_____

2. Who will help you learn the MLS?

_____

_____

_____

3. What are the markets you need to learn and watch?

_____

_____

_____

_____

Additional Notes

_____

_____

_____

_____

_____

_____

~ 5 ~

The Analysis

As a real estate investor, there are three different types of analyses—personal, property, financial or the marketplace—to perform before entering a transaction. To be successful these three analyses should be completed each time you move into a new purchase.

Previously in this book we have touched on each area, but will now offer additional detail in the form of questions to ask yourself during each analysis phase.

Personal

Long before a property analysis is complete, it is recommended to perform a self-analysis.

Much of the knowledge and wherewithal comes from and within you. Only you can determine the criteria and data you wish to use.

◊ What's My Risk Tolerance?

As an investor, your risk tolerance depends on how much change you can stomach during the massive market swings that can occasionally occur, and being able to survive through the turmoil.

Risk tolerance could include the following considerations:

- The amount of your cash liquidity or how much money you have available for investments
- Your total net worth
- Your age and investment horizon
- How soon you need the cash you invest to offer a return
- Your investment partners considerations
- How much money you can afford to lose on a transaction without altering your wealth trajectory

Of course, no one wants to lose money. But as an investor, that's a risk you undertake. Some losses can cripple your real estate investment business while others can be considered manageable or insignificant, in relation to your financial position.

Understanding the ebb and flow of real estate values and pricing will help to avoid panic settling in and forcing your hand to buy or sell too quickly.

You also want to ensure you don't take on too much—or too many properties—at any given time.

It is also helpful to know there are two types of investors: aggressive and conservative. An aggressive investor is one who has a high level of tolerance in that he or she is willing to lose money to gain results or profit. The conservative investor operates at low tolerance, making investments that will maintain his or her original investment.

What type of investor am I?

A. Aggressive
B. Conservative

◊ What Resources Do I Need?

Of course, the number one resource to acquire is money in the bank, cash on hand. This resource will make it easy for buying decisions without having to rely on outside sources.

However, having those outside resources can be beneficial in times of uncertainty or unexpected surprises that can happen with a property, as well as in your personal life.

Playing into the theory of having outside resources is something called *economies to scale*. While you grow your investor career and your properties increase over time, you will have a better chance to lower your costs because of more people involved in the particular process.

Outside resources can also be members of your already established team discussed in chapter 3, such as realtors, contractors, and bankers.

Other resources are necessary to comfortably function as a real estate investor. They include research and informative, investigative, and online tools, such as Loopnet, MorningReport, MLS, or BiggerPockets.com.

However, most of these come with a premium tied to them and can be costly. But if you are to join my reasonably priced Shared Equity Program, you would have all these programs and more available to use at no extra cost to you. More on that later.

A good question for you to ask yourself might be what resources do I have to have to complete this transaction comfortably? A partial list of items is shown below. What other resources can you think of?

- Cash on hand
- Outside resources (realtor, contractors, bankers)
- MLS
- Online support tools and reports

◊ What Skills Do I Bring to the Table?

Irrefutably, having several skill sets is imperative when it comes to running any business.

Be Personable

Being in a career where you have daily contact with the general public, you must be a people person.

Being in relationship with someone is different than if you are IN a relationship. However, maybe not that much, as you still must be able to talk, negotiate, and work with that person. The ability to converse and be comfortable in talking with people is the number one skill that you must possess.

What never ceases to amaze me when hosting trainings on building relationships is the number of individuals who are afraid to speak up or do not know how to strike up a conversation with another person.

If you are uncomfortable with putting yourself out there, practice is the only way to get over this fear. Putting that fear to bed is one reason why I offer a class to gain the skill of getting comfortable with people, so you can create the relationships necessary as an investor.

Be Knowledgeable

Do your homework. Knowing about property, the real estate market, or knowing where to find answers and being able to research all angles of real estate, is a great skill. Not everyone will take the time to learn, nor do they have the patience.

Know How to Negotiate

Negotiation is another essential skill to have as a real estate investor.

A successful negotiation happens from the confidence you have in what you know about the situation and circumstance at hand. If not careful, you could find yourself being talked down to a price other than which you are willing to sell, or up to a price at which you do not wish to buy.

And so, having the knowledge before going into a negotiation setting will boost your confidence and guarantee a successful outcome.

Control Emotions

Lastly to mention here, but indeed, not the end of the skills list is being able to control your emotions. As a new investor, you may get caught up in an extraordinary opportunity during the first few months of your new career. But as you may know, all logic goes out the window when emotions come to play.

Being able to remove yourself from the dollar and cents flashing in your head to consider the proposition, after completing a proper analysis, is a skill worth developing.

Real estate is not about emotion, except to the end-user. The best strategy is a disciplined approach.

What skills do I need to work on most?

    A. People skills
    B. Research skills
    C. Negotiation skills
    D. Hold emotions in check skills

Property

Completing a property analysis helps to determine several factors, including which lender to use for financing, if necessary. The analysis will also determine other costs, such as repairs and agent fees.

Also through the analysis you will deduce a good investment opportunity from a bad one, and the length of your investment—short-term of a year or less, or long-term, one year to five years or even longer.

Once you decide the type of property in which to invest, completing a thorough analysis thereafter, it is then recommended to employ the following influences.

◊ Use Your Team

As mentioned in chapter 3, having a team that has expertise and knowledge in their respective fields can help you achieve a profitable transaction, especially, up front and in the analysis stage of the property.

- Your lawyer is to provide legal advice, prepare necessary documents, deeds
- Your accountant should be good at money management, disbursement of funds at appropriate times
- Contractors who offer repair estimates specific to their occupation
- Real estate agents to assist with property values and potential buyers

◊ Set Minimum Price

Some investors look for properties to buy and hold, and other investors are constantly in the buy-sell mode.

Interestingly enough, the profit on the property is determined when you purchase the property, and not when you sell the property. The price is determined by what you propose to do with it—keep it for a rental or turn the property for a profit.

As a rule, however, most investors use the 70% formula, which is that of the original cost of the property, plus repair costs, which must be no greater than 70% of the potential sale price of the property.

For example, the property is $300,000 to purchase. After repairs and other costs it can be sold at $400,000, falling within the 70% rule.

Most investors use this same information to determine whether they acquire property or not, allowing for contingencies, in anticipation of realizing a desired amount of profit.

If the property does not fall under this 70% rule in setting the price, it is advisable to leave it alone and not move forward with the purchase.

Ensure Lender Guidelines for Funding are Met

Each lender has their criteria when it comes to lending money. The big banks have their sweet spots based on credit and markets. However, all commercial banks and savings associations are encouraged through the Community Reinvestment Act of 1977 to help meet the needs of local areas and neighborhoods, in acting favorably to all who apply, and not just those from wealthy backgrounds and markets.

What does this have to do with completing a property analysis? It is important to know what each lender's rules and guidelines are before assessing a property. For if none of the banks you work with would invest in a piece of real estate you are looking at, then you may need to pass up this particular opportunity.

◊ Marketplace

Your real estate agents can be put to good use while completing an analysis on what is available because they are knowledgeable and adept at going through the MLS to find properties for you. As an individual, if you go to the MLS, you may not easily understand all the information it contains, much less be able to process that information.

When seeking out property, you should have a general idea of what interests you.

Here are a few parameters to consider.

Purchase Price to Sell Price Ratio

As previously mentioned, having determined a percentage of the purchase and selling price, with a firm estimate of costs pitched in, is a wise practice to establish. This method has the potential to mitigate the risk of your investments.

Turnaround Time

If not quite yet seasoned in the investing field, your team will be able to give you firm estimates with regards to timing with repairs and also how long the property will be on the market once it is ready for the next steps. A thorough analysis completed on similar property bought and sold in the area will offer the information necessary to make a good decision.

Research Lenders

Knowing what your lenders need for financing before going into a transaction is most helpful. Some lenders, and you will learn more in chapter 6 of this book, have different criteria based on the type of property. The lender is the person bringing money to the table. They too need to complete an analysis (assessment), if you would be a good fit with whom to work.

Summary

There are many points to consider before performing a complete analysis when making an investment. Below are a few questions to ask during the process.

- What type of investor am I?
- What resources do I have to complete this transaction comfortably alone?
- What personal skills do I need to work on most?
- What am I willing to commit to in becoming a real estate investor?
- What team members need to be in place when considering a property?
- What is the purchase to sell ratio to which I will set and adhere?
- What is the maximum turnaround time that makes the most sense when considering a property?
- Would it be wiser to seek a partner for this project?
- Should I explore this property with my mentor/coach before proceeding?

Notes & Review

This section is for your use to make note of any ideas that came to you while reading the chapter.

This section will also contain questions that were asked within the chapter. Space has been provided for you to record your answers.

1. Using the list in the summary section answer the questions using the space below, continuing on the next page.

_____

_____

Additional Notes

_____

_____

_____

_____

_____

_____

_____

_____

_____

_____

_____

_____

_____

_____

_____

_____

_____

_____

~ 6 ~

The Financing

Financing is simple, not complicated. However, it is highly recommended you be well-versed and educated before seeking any financing on your transactions.

Types of Financing

There are three types of money when talking about real estate investing: cash reserve, private funding, and conventional funding.

With each model, having a few hand-selected financiers on your team who have different areas of lending expertise and monies available is a wise decision.

◊ Cash Reserve

The cash reserve model is for the people who have significant cash liquidity, that is, the ability to turn assets easily into cash. These sources may include money from previous investing or other sources—such as insurance, lawsuits, inheritance, or settlements—to initialize a transaction.

◊ Private Funding

The private funding which includes shared equity is available from sources such as individuals who are independently wealthy and lend to people seeking to do the same in real estate without the need for direct involvement. In other words, their money is now working for them. Some persons or companies with less financial capacity may pool resources to accomplish the same objective. Hedge funds are also a great source for private real estate investment.

Private funds are generally asset based and not dependent on credit. Private lenders require, depending on experience and relationships, anywhere from 10-50% of your money, and this is in addition to the closing costs associated with the transaction. Closing costs can range from 2-10% of the purchase price. The remainder of costs usually are funded by the private lender.

A Word about Our Shared Equity Program

Our training and education program will provide access to many of these funding resources to enable and expedite your success when applying the principles we teach. This program applies to you who, as a new investor, has little or no money to use, but possesses the desire to get started with real estate investing. A successful investor can identify the right investment opportunity in the right location with the right margins for the specific investors with whom you seek to work.

You may have money available, but not enough to initialize or to start a transaction independently. There are financial resources available that are willing to share the costs of the money needed to buy a property, and thereby, having mutual interest and equity in the process.

Our company can provide access to resources you need as part of the Shared Equity Program to start your real estate business. You will have an opportunity to learn much more about this process and how it can help you.

◊ Conventional Funding

Conventional funding is usually available to those who have good credit and sufficient assets. Types of collateral might be cash, other real estate, negotiable stocks, or bonds. To obtain financing through a traditional lender, the collateral must be worth enough to support your real estate investment needs, all the while meeting the lender's requirements.

This type of funding requires you to have 10-30% of your funds for a transaction, and the lending institution will fund the remainder.

Note that interest rates are not quoted here because they fluctuate with the marketplace—however, standard loan rates are lower than the private rates.

Misconceptions about Lenders

Let's talk about lenders and the big misunderstanding around them and money.

◊ Unlimited Funds

Most people think the lenders have millions and millions of dollars they are sitting on, ready for the investor just for the asking. The investor may believe they can take their time to analyze the transaction and that the money will be there and available when ready to move forward. But this is not always the case. At some point in time lenders could cap out.

Lenders have access to money just as real estate investors have access, with credit lines and cash on reserve. However, it is the timing that is important as to when the money is available. You see, a lender makes money by moving that money into the marketplace, turning it over with points and interest.

Here's an example. You may come to an investor with a property. The investor's liquidity—or availability to cash—may not, however, accommodate another transaction (yours) at that moment. The cash may be ready a day or two later, but you need the money now.

Therefore, it is essential for investors to have multiple lenders and lending resources in his or her portfolio to tap and access.

◊ Unlimited Time

Let's also talk about timing where lenders are concerned.

As stated earlier, an investor needs to move money to make money. The quicker an investor can turn money the more money he or she makes.

It is everybody's idea in this game to make as much money as they can and as quickly as they can. Markets can change, and relatively quickly. You will not want to get caught with too many assets and no liquidity. For if that happens, you can choke.

If you get caught with too much money and no assets, then the market slows, and you also have problems with turning over the cash.

Lenders, especially, must have a very keen sense of the market and be able to balance the money and assets to get through that process.

Types of Lenders

Investors have funds to infuse while real estate professionals have assets to sell straight out or rehabilitate for a later sale. Given those positions, the two have a way of being able to come together when the circumstances are right.

The lender has terms and conditions or certain "sweet spots." Big lenders may have favorable factors around credit, credit ratings, or around specific markets. A creditor may want to work in certain markets but may not want to work in others. At the federal level, as in public banks, some laws dictate that the lenders lend in all markets. Private lenders, however, are not subjected to the same constraints.

This description may be a bit confusing to you right now, but read on for further clarification.

◊ Public

Lenders considered to be public are those institutions that lend money based on assets carried by checking and savings account holders, plus impose predetermined fees.

Charter Limitations

All agencies operate under a charter which outline and define a corporate body's rights and privileges. Some organizations are also governed not only by their charter but that of an upper branch controlling certain assets, for instance. And for this reason, public lenders may be limited in loaning money for real estate investment purposes.

Also, banks have strict regulations when it comes to loaning money to small businesses, whether or not they are new, established, or growing. It stands to reason for the public banks to protect their members' assets against the possibility of losing money loaned to borrowers with high credit risk.

◊ Private

Private lenders are businesses that deal only in lending money for the sole purpose of making money. Their interest rates may be greater than public banks, but worth the cost if obtaining the loan can start your real estate investing career.

Greater & Quicker Access to Money

Private lenders also have some limitations regarding the footprint they can cover. But generally, these lenders possess greater and quicker access to available funds due to not having the same restrictions as the public or institutional lenders do when lending money.

Therefore, for a lot of reasons, our company deals primarily with private funders—or lenders.

Some private lenders will have programs that they make available to the investor and operate in a particular arena where they have a good understanding of the market—and where the market will present a low risk. The more sophisticated private lenders offer programs to guide the investor through that market risk and returns process, covering broader markets.

Short-Term Loans

In the chapter on analysis, we spoke briefly about short-term loans, and how they are anywhere between one and twelve months, but may extend to thirty-six months for larger projects or new construction development. Lenders who offer short-term loans have different criteria for lending money. Some do interest-only loans but will also charge points for those transactions.

Points are given in exchange to reduce the interest rate. For example, 1 point = 1%; 2 points = 2%. Therefore, on a $100,000 loan, you could borrow the money at 7% interest, plus 1 point, or $1,000. To get an even lower rate you may consider the loan at 6% interest, plus $2,000.

Portfolio Loans

While most real estate investors buy and sell, some buy and hold property to build up their asset account. A few lenders will support this type of activity. However, the properties must be producing, meaning the investor should have the liquidity to carry those properties. For if they are not able to bear the costs, the lenders will not put themselves at risk.

As a new investor, you want to build your asset portfolio. Also as a new investor, you may have the instinct to obtain a loan on your entire portfolio to get a few hundred thousand dollars in return. This type of action is a risk you may not want to take. If something goes wrong with the current transaction, you could lose everything.

How to Find Private Lenders

There are private lenders in almost any market. What is the best way to find and connect with a private lender? I always suggest first to look online, using the phrase "private real estate funders" or "lenders" in the search field to obtain the best results.

If you were to be involved with a shared equity program, such as the one I offer, you have unlimited access to the many tiers of lenders in our pool. The benefit here is that if a transaction does not work with one lender, you move on to another until the funding is approved.

Another way to find private lenders is by talking to local real estate attorneys. They should be on your team and can provide a deep pocket of private resources available, and perhaps, unknown to the general public.

One additional lending channel is an institution heralded as a "capital resource," otherwise known as a "hard money lender." This type of lender, again, operates under different terms and regulations than the conventional banks. Capital resource lenders realize the needs of the real estate investor, and especially when it comes to money that is not required to just purchase the property, but also to cover costs of rehabilitation.

Establish a Relationship with Private Lenders

After an evaluation of potential private lenders, the next step in the process is to determine which ones are suitable for you as an investor. Determine for each lender what the rates and terms are, what products they accept, their lending limitations, and what types of loans they service.

Most lenders have a loan originator, also known as a loan scout, to put money in the marketplace. Once you, as the prospective real estate investor, decides on the process—the plan—and hopefully after completing a full evaluation, you can call upon a lender to confirm the terms and conditions of obtaining a loan.

If the initial meeting is affable, an appointment to meet with the originator from the agency would be the next step. That loan originator can then share insight with you before a transaction begins, and also about the likelihood of funding, based on the location of the property and its return on investment.

Know Your Money-Backers

While seeking money for your transaction, you must look for the right person or place that will fund your project, and sometimes, there can be more than one. You may have someone who is willing to offer a shared equity stake for part of the transaction and also a lender who will make up the difference—which is the very reason why, as an investor, to have multiple streams of revenue available in your toolbox.

One of the tools you will need during the financing process is one you learned about in previous chapters: develop relationships. Getting to know someone who could put up the cash and move through the transaction process relatively quickly and easily is someone who you want to know.

Having choices of several lenders in your arsenal will increase your chance to secure financing. (Our programs provide you access to many different lenders serving many markets across the U.S.)

Of course, not everything sent to a creditor will meet their criteria. If you submit a proposal for a loan request to one lender, but the margins are very tight, you might be able to go to a more risk-tolerant lender to obtain funding.

Should I Use My Money?

As stated in chapter 3, the best practice, especially as a new investor, is to buy and sell property procuring enough cash that will make future investing decisions easier and comfortably.

Keep in mind that comfort levels vary from investor to investor. What is right for one may not be on the same level for the other.

For instance, $200,000 of liquidity may be enough to look at a property, but $500,000 liquidity can be enough to both purchase and rehab it. However, in another market where property values are less, $200,000 may just suffice that level of comfort.

Even though this may be the case, you still want to exercise caution when using your money. Borrowing money, when possible, can avoid depleting your personal resources should any catastrophic, unexpected events arise.

3 Secrets of Financing

Waiting to do the research on a lender after you locate a property to purchase could result in the loss of acquiring it. Therefore, before you begin or continue with your investing career, consider the following three secrets to secure financing successfully.

◊ Secret #1

The first step is to identify lenders, along with their terms and conditions. By applying this approach, you are three steps ahead than perhaps another investor who is looking at the same piece of real estate.

You want to have a lender involved from stage one in your process because they are going to help you package the deal. If you try to do the transaction alone, you will more than likely fall short with some of the anticipated costs. Without some guidance, these institutions are very quick to reject a request if everything is not in place.

Getting lenders on your team before you begin as an investor, should be your first step.

◊ Secret #2

Once you have a list of potential lenders, examine their mission and vision statements. If you are the type of real estate investor who wants to make a few hundred thousand bucks, you will not want to look at lenders that want to improve communities. The reverse is true as well. If you are socially and economically responsible, you may not want to work with a lender who is in business only to make fast money.

Let's say you are passionate about being in the real estate arena—then that is the criteria you want to pursue when looking for a lender.

You will want to keep in mind that these three types of investors and lenders—socially stimulated, money motivated, and passion driven—could work across the aisle. Everything depends on the plan you lay out in the beginning.

◊ Secret #3

The third secret to a successful financing is to build your cash reserve. The worry of losing the deal of the century because you lack lenders or funders who won't back you would be non-existent if you had money of your own in the bank to use.

Setting up a plan to build your financial resources for future transactions is not only essential but a critical factor when it comes to secrets of financing for the real estate investor.

A Word of Warning

Never seek to finance in desperation or without your team. Some unscrupulous lenders will set loans up for failure. They do this by creating language within the lending contract in such a way that brings certainty to breach the contract. You then become the likely candidate for their foreclosure on your asset.

The following are examples of how lenders can bilk you out of your property.

1. Your loan contract says your payment is due on the first of the month, but there is mention of a grace period. By paying your mortgage on the second of the month, or after that, you have breached your contract.
2. Your lending entity has multiple locations, and they direct you to pay at a particular location on a specific date. If you do not comply with either stipulation, you've breached your contract.
3. If your lender requires a comprehensive policy with liability and you acquire a fire policy—as with a vacant property—which is the only coverage most insurers provide, you would be in breach of your contract.
4. If your lending contract stipulates that your taxes, water, and sewer bills be kept current and you become thirty days delinquent on the bill, you are in breach of your contract.

I mention the preceding only because investors outside of our training program have brought these situations to us in search of solutions to avoid foreclosure. And while we were able to help some, others were not so fortunate due to having other intentions and would not cooperate.

These situations are especially common when your asset has lots of equity or profit to be gained.

Do not feel obligated to sign any such contract, and especially, if your legal counsel brings it to your attention. It may be better to walk away from that transaction, lose the deposit or the opportunity than to undertake the transaction—having to deal with the subsequent loss of time, energy, and resources it would take to fight through the process with any measure of success. It is a losing proposition.

Summary

The process of obtaining financing is as crucial as the real estate transaction itself.

- Make cash fast to build your reserve, safeguarding liquidity
- Research lenders and funders who are in alignment with your mission and vision values
- Build and maintain those relationships
- Be wary of lending contract language
- Have multiple lenders and funders on your team that accommodates different investing scenarios

For free, detailed instructions on how to obtain financing, go to http://GenuineRealEstateInvestingMadeEasy.com
to receive immediate access.

Notes & Review

This section is for your use to make note of any ideas that came to you while reading the chapter.

This section will also contain questions that were asked within the chapter. Space has been provided for you to record your answers.

1. Where should I look for a private lender?

_____

_____

_____

2. What resources do I have to have to complete a transaction comfortably?

_____

_____

_____

_____

3. Should I use my own money? Why or why not?

_____

_____

_____

_____

Additional Notes

_____

_____

_____

_____

_____

_____

_____

_____

~ 7 ~

The Rehab Process

This book is for the investor seeking residential rehab properties. These types of real estate investments relate to selecting property 1) bought at or below market price, 2) needing renovations, and 3) sold at a marginal profit.

Not What You See on Television

These days many television programs are sensationalizing and showcasing houses that need to be fixed or brought up to code and habitable standards of its locality. Because this type of programming is on television, they use behind the scenes magic like maneuvers and activities that do not happen in the actual environment of flipping or rehab transactions. What you see is not the reality of real estate.

In fact with rehab realty property, you are not going to buy a house to flip in only two days unless it just needs painting. I know a lot of folks who watch these television programs only to get excited at the possibility of making huge profits. What you don't see on television is that these types of flips are orchestrated, three or four of them at a time, and by the same group of people for different audiences.

◊ Unforeseen Challenges

The other piece to what you see on TV is not, in reality, the actual process, and which is likely much more cumbersome. There are many moving parts of the rehab process because of the many people involved and where a lot can go wrong: underestimations, overestimations, or conditions you didn't see or notice on the first inspection. This includes anything that is under the surface of a home, and where significant structural problems exist, such as damage created by termites.

◊ Importance of a Team

Although I am not a home inspector, I was once a general contractor. During that brief time, I became aware of the hidden dangers that lent to that knowledge of what could be lurking sight unseen.

Therefore, and I cannot say this enough, the most important aspect of being a real estate investor is to have the right team members in place. Having experienced people looking at the property to get a good understanding of any challenges you may face is wise. They can help determine the probability of profit from the transaction by noting problems that may be hidden from the untrained eye.

Steps to Rehab a Property

Once you research the market and locate a property in an area and condition that you, as an investor, feel confident and competent in working through for a profit, then you can continue your analysis work. As a new investor, however, I would recommend finding a property that is not a major rehab, such as one requiring plumbing, heating, or electrical work—but finding an opportunity where a property needs a bit of painting and minor carpentry.

You will find that patience is a constant requirement in the real estate investment arena. Rushing into the wrong transaction just to do a transaction can be costly and counterproductive, and sometimes, devastating.

Be patient and be diligent in your research and outreach and your opportunity will arise.

◊ Complete the Property Analysis

Once you have the property selected, you are ready to continue with the rest of the analysis and prepare your timetable regarding contractor visits, inspections, estimate turnarounds, and other affairs necessary to ensure timely execution of property disposition. After you place a deposit on the property, of which I recommend only a few hundred dollars at most, write up a contract with the seller creating a timeline for you to do your due diligence on lining up the rest of your team.

I recommend only a few hundred dollars at most because legally one dollar can be considered a good faith gesture since it is legal tender currency. However, and in many cases, real estate agents and brokers will insist you make larger deposits to demonstrate deeper faith by risking more money to indicate you are not wasting their time.

In the case of the seller who does not stipulate a specific deposit in the listing, as a buyer, you can make a deposit with which you are comfortable. Do not be pushed into making a deposit of thousands of dollars to satisfy the wishes of a real estate agent. The more money you put towards the deposit, the more money you tend to lose if the transaction becomes contentious, and in which sometimes they can.

◊ Allow Time for Due Diligence

According to Merriam-Webster.com ["Due Diligence." Merriam-

Webster.com. Merriam-Webster, n.d. Web. 12 Dec. 2016.], due diligence refers to "research and analysis of a company or organization done in preparation for a business transaction (as a corporate merger or purchase of securities)."

As it relates to real estate, due diligence may include, but not be limited to, the examination of property with experienced professionals of their field in obtaining adequate information to determine if:

- Physical condition and construction of the property renders it suitable for acquisition and further suitable for your portfolio and experience
- Title is clean and will allow clear conveyance
- Mechanical, electrical, heating, and plumbing including septic systems are serviceable or replaced
- Roof structure and its integrity, as well as the roof covering, is sound and sturdy

You must also endeavor to assess the curb appeal—color and landscape—since these will factor quite high in the resale of your property.

Also, exterior concerns should include ensuring that trees are not leaning on or over the roof surface or in proximity to it.

Check that there are no hazardous wires or surfaces or drainage that would adversely impact the property or its occupants.

You will also want to inspect and test for hazardous gasses or environmental threats, such as mold and other fungi, are not found in the property and that it has adequate ventilation systems.

I would suggest setting the amount to complete your research for at least twenty (20) days to have all of your inspections completed, with your facts and figures in place. If the project is small, fifteen (15) days might suffice. However, if the project is on the larger side, thirty (30) days would be a better allowance—and one you may want to set as a rule of thumb for every transaction.

This timeframe includes getting all the repair estimates back from your team so you can make an informed decision when all is said and done to purchase the property.

◊ Obtain Team with Specialized Areas

You put the deposit down on the property. You gain agreement with the seller with the caveat of obtaining favorable review and reports from your inspectors. You set a due diligence period of twenty (20) or thirty (30) days. The more days you allow for, the more time you have to find contractors and inspectors who can give a thorough evaluation of the property. (This, too, cannot be reiterated often enough!)

Now it's time to get to work. The best and most efficient strategy is to get the team of those who will be completing the inspections there on the same day. That way you will not be wasting your time going back and forth to the property at various times throughout this period.

It can take about one to three hours, depending on the size and complexity of the property, for a contractor or inspector on your team to walk through the property and gather his or her notes. You will want to give yourself time with each to review those notes just in case you have any questions on the spot.

It is wise and recommended to schedule each of your team members two hours apart on the day of the property's visit. Starting at eight or nine o'clock in the morning is not out of line for the inspections to begin, for you will be there most of the day.

Depending on the property and the condition it is in, you may only need a few of your team for evaluation purposes. Let's review the team members that should, but not limited to, be there.

Structural Contractors

You want someone who can look at a property and see items that may be a potential cause of concern and considerable financial cost regarding repairs. Basement walls, for instance, that are damp may be due to more than just a heavy rain. A roof that has a lot of debris may be rotting underneath.

Pest Control

Carpenter ants and other varmints which are visible around the property can indicate the structure is damaged. Having a team member versed in this category along with the structural contractor can ease potential threats of damage and devise a plan to control the pests.

Zoning Administrators

Occasionally, there might be issues about a permitting or zoning level. For instance, if the property is a single or two family house, but you seek to turn it into a three family house, you will want someone who can advise you on the logistics, probability, and the tax implications. Even if you do not want to change the house capacity, checking in with a zoning administer about the property would still be recommended.

Building Inspectors

If the property is visually in need of repair, it may mean that it is not up to code. A building inspector will be able to give you a list of items that need to be fixed to bring the property to a standard of habitability, according to the local codes.

Architects

Dependent upon the level of restoration and renovation you envision, I always recommend there is a draftsman on site the day of inspection. And if you can find the original architect or plan of the property that would be all the better. However, not in all cases will it be a likely occurrence.

◊ **Estimate the Profit Margin**

In most cases, you will receive the estimates from each of your contractors and inspectors between seven and ten days.

From the estimates you will determine if there is enough margin to make a profit—that is, how much you can make on the sale of the property once all the figures are received.

Another person with whom to confer is someone who can give you a "broker price opinion (BPO)." That someone could be a real estate agent, appraiser, or another qualified person. The professional can provide an estimate on what the value of the property might be after all the rehab repairs are complete.

Your estimated margin of profit is calculated using the following formula:

Profit Margin = BPO - Purchase Price - Rehab Costs

You may also calculate the profit percentage by this formula:

Profit Percentage = (Net Profit / Cost Price) x 100%

Different people are comfortable with different levels of what they call profit. Somebody may make a 10% profit and be satisfied with that outcome. For example, a transaction completes at $250,000. The profit margin ends up at $25,000. This person is ecstatic with that dollar amount. Some of the seasoned investors, however, will see that as very marginal, i.e., not enough, and may want to adjust their original purchase offer or other numbers to increase the margin of profit.

The importance of knowing your profit margin number is to assist lenders with the decision to loan out money. If the profit margin or percentage, such as the above example, is small according to the lending institution's standards, they may see the transaction as a risk and, therefore, deny your loan application. Twenty-five thousand dollars may seem like a lot of money to you, but can quickly be eaten up by undisclosed or unforeseen rehab costs.

Again, however, this is where the importance of having a reliable and trusted team working for you comes into play. If your contractors, inspectors, and other team members are schooled and experienced in their fields, then a 10% profit margin may satisfy both you and the bank.

However, in cases where the deal does not go through, pick up stakes, contact your real estate agent to see what property is next on the list, and move forward with the new knowledge packed in your back pocket.

Obtain Titles, Deeds, Permits & More

When the purchase is approved, the paperwork continues and becomes more involved and important. You will not only be working with the above team members, but you will also now retain your attorney to assist in the legal matters of property ownership, such as title and deed.

◊ Obtain Clear Title or Deed

While completing the analysis and estimating the margin profit you want to ensure there are no liens against the property—and if there are, determine what kind. Many lien types are available that could interfere with your purchase.

There is the general bank note or mortgage. The property could also have a deed of trust, whereby a trustee holds the title as security for a loan. Also, there could be a hold from past due and unpaid taxes— either property or income tax liens from the Internal Revenue Service. Other common types could include contractor liens, unpaid alimony, child support payments, or any other judgments placed on the property.

The best type of property to look for is one that carries or holds a "warranty deed." A warranty deed ensures the buyer that the seller holds a title clear of any and all liens. However, and in some states such as Massachusetts, they offer a quit-claim deed which has similar terms to a warranty deed.

◊ Contract with your Contractors

Once the closing is over, you will want to start the repairs on the property. Your contractor should always provide you with a timeline. Here is where you will contract with your contractors.

The process is not just a handwritten piece of paper that says your guys are going to do this, this, and this. An actual plan or schedule of what repairs and by what date they will be completed should be received from the contractor.

For instance, phase 1 of the work will be the installation of the kitchen cabinets. Phase 2 is the bathroom rework of the tile, flooring, tub and shower, and new fixtures. Phase 3 might be all the painting throughout the house, done to touch up the look and give a fresh new feel to the place.

If you have ever had work done of any kind on your home, especially construction work, you know that the crew has more than just your job, often running from one site to the next during the day. You want to ensure those who work for you carry out the work on your property on time and within budget.

You may also want to get a commitment from your contractors that the crew assigned to work on your property will not be reassigned until your job has completed. Adding performance deadlines—with financial consequences if not met—is a wise practice to start from the get-go. (Because creating contracts of this type can be a daunting task, I coach, at length, on how to create them in my training.)

A Note about Funds Payout

Although this is a discussion that could have been in the finance chapter, I thought it would best serve you here.

The funding for your transaction, in most cases, will come from a lender. The amount of money that is made available to you covers both the acquisition and the repair of the property. Banks will release funds for 1) the initial purchase, and 2) at each benchmark determined by the contractor.

In other words, the money needed to buy the property gets distributed first. Then, as each construction phase completes, as stated in the contract, the lender will release those funds.

Depending on your lender you may be charged interest for the loan one of two ways: on the full amount (purchase price + repair costs), or on the use of the money, as it is doled out at the end of each phase completion. The former is where a consequence clause comes in handy if the work is not complete in time:

"If a work phase goes over the time allotted a penalty of X amount of dollars will be imposed." This action may save you from paying additional interest fees and places the burden on the contractor.

◊ Obtain Building/Construction Permits

Building and construction permits are necessary and required in most jurisdictions. Please note if you do not acquire a building permit the increased value, which could be realized from your repairs and improvement, may not be pointed out in an appraisal, and could adversely affect the value you would realize on the sale of the property. The permit application is the only method that jurisdiction authorities have of getting information about the improvement and making it a part of the public record. They are issued at the local level so that the work done is in compliance with all building codes. If, however, you forgo obtaining a building permit you could be liable for fines and at worst, deconstruction of any work completed.

Having a formal contract with your construction crew will be a huge benefit when applying for these permits. Putting work into fixing up a property will only add to the assessed value.

Most people, however, will try to gauge the real value above the assessed value. In some cases, they are very close, yet in other instances, it may be a great difference between them. But the bottom line is you will only get credit for the repairs and restoration if there is a permit that says the work is complete.

Summary

At the beginning of this book, we talked about the importance of having a plan. Creating a step-by-step schedule of tasks can make the process of a rehab easy and straightforward.

Below is a recap of the procedural steps to take.

- Forget everything you've seen on TV about buying and fixing up houses
- Get your contractors, real estate agents, attorneys, and other team members in place and at the ready
- Complete a thorough analysis of the property using your team specialized in different areas of expertise, allowing enough time for the reports and estimates to come back for review
- Calculate your profit margin, both in dollars and in percentage
- Obtain necessary papers, such as a clear deed and title
- Upon closing, get the appropriate building and construction permits
- Follow the work in close collaboration to ensure all repairs finish on schedule

Notes & Review

This section is for your use to make note of any ideas that came to you while reading the chapter.

This section will also contain questions that were asked within the chapter. Space has been provided for you to record your answers.

1. What is the best procedure to complete a property analysis?

_____

_____

_____

_____

_____

2. Who do I need on my team that can help give an accurate estimate of repairs?

_____

_____

_____

_____

3. What else do I need to have in place during the rehab process?

_____

_____

_____

_____

Additional Notes

_____

_____

_____

_____

_____

_____

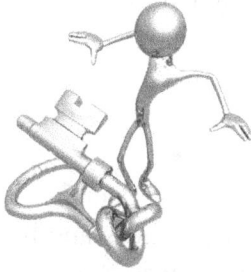

~ 8 ~

The Conundrum

Now that you have gone to all that work and effort in fixing up your investment property, you may be saying to yourself, "Gee. This house looks pretty nice. I may want to think about moving here myself!"

Before you make a hasty decision to relocate, there are a few items to consider.

Smart Navigation Tactics

In chapter 4 we discussed the consideration of either hanging on to the property as an income source or selling it for the straight profit option. You may remember as well that as a new investor, I suggest taking the time to learn the ropes, to get the feel of the real estate investing business, and that slow and steady wins the race.

Although you plan in the same way, each transaction can be entirely different from the other. Therefore, the more experience you have, the better and the more savvy you become. And with all that experience also comes more property and opportunity in renovating homes that catch your eye.

What I will not suggest is that you don't buy the first property you rehab. I will not dominate your decision-making in that way. I can only counsel you on best practices and the knowledge I've gained from time-after-time experiences.

Let's take this opportunity, however, to circle back to the tactical and practical pieces of being a real estate investor.

◊ Revisit Goals

There is an entire preparation phase to complete before you even look at the property. You need to know your overall objectives during this process. To figure them out, review these five points and then ask yourself "the" question.

Duration

What is your intention with real estate investing with regards to the length you plan to be in the business arena? Will you be in it for the long haul? Perhaps you are thinking short-term—just make a few quick bucks, get out, and do something else?

The question: Are you in real estate investing for the long-haul or short-term?

Motivation

What is the catalyst, the driver that which led you to this occupational choice? Is it for reasons of money, family, independence, to improve communities, putting people to work so they, too, can have financial success?

The question: What is your stimulant—your why?

Aspiration

What do you want to be when you grow up? What legacy do you

wish to leave behind? What do you want to accomplish now, at this point in your life? Is it to have extra income, financial freedom, or more time with family?

The question: What do you wish to achieve?

Gratification

In what do you excel? What can you do that no one else can? Are you good at talking with people? Do you have a knack for making others feel comfortable in your presence? What is the one thing you love to do?

The question: What are your strengths?

Disinclination

This last piece of the puzzle is to hone in on the things you don't want to do. It is also the time to admit to the stuff at which you aren't good.

The question: What are your weakest points?

The above alliterations will assist with recall. The main idea, however, is for you to create your phrases or words that will bring to mind this whole self-assessment process when reviewing your goals and the questions which need asking.

◊ Stick to the Plan

Just as an architect designs a blueprint to erect a building that is stable and secure, so would you develop a structure that will accommodate successful transactions over time.

Initially, if you are cash poor and don't have money to invest yourself, your initial plan could be is to have a formal written arrangement with someone for whom you can do research and share in the transaction profit until you accumulate enough funds to work independently.

Conversely, if you have sufficient funds to invest independently and you use your funds to buy and hold property, you may have lots of property and equity but no liquidity, which is not a good position.

Therefore, and as suggested, consider your needs as well as that of your family, and develop a plan that will create success to your satisfaction and beyond. If you have difficulty doing this, there are coaches and mentors (me included) who are always willing to help out, once getting to know your needs and your capacity.

By completing the self-assessment questions above is the first step of the plan to which you should refer. Then you want to make sure your desired outcomes remain as when you began.

As mentioned earlier in this book, my plan was to have homes congruent with my growing family. Being able to buy and sell real estate as an investor satisfied that plan.

If you are in the real estate investing arena to make a quick few hundred thousand dollars, then you may have in your plan that you will not buy and hold property. Quick turnarounds could very well give you what you desire.

But if you are taking advantage of the long-term opportunity REI provides as a life-long career the plan should contain steps and processes that which leads to that end.

Whichever plan you choose to follow, you and your family can live a life never imagined. Having a plan and sticking to it is what leads to success.

But what happens if while re-examining the process you discover something has changed in the scheme? You do not need to worry. By following the same process of revisiting your plan prior to the execution of each transaction will allow for adjustments, if warranted, to be made.

◊ Build Equity

One of the most important objectives to have in the real estate investing business is to accumulate your bank account as quickly and efficiently as possible. The more equity you have, the easier it can be to obtain bank loans, most certainly, but also remove the worry of not having enough resources for unexpected expenses.

If you do not stick to the plan as suggested above, you run the risk of developing bad habits. Over time, the decision to change up the original plan can choke you. Should you have more assets than cash liquidity, you also run the risk of missing an opportunity because you need time to convert the asset to the amount of liquid cash necessary to make a purchase.

To buy and sell property is a good strategy to implement until you reach a certain level of liquidity. You decide what that number is but at a minimum I recommend $200,000 for a beginning investor. And that amount is set aside for your business. You may want to continue with the buy-sell process until you reach $500,000 so you can have a safety net for your family as well.

Continue to turn and grow your money with each transaction. Set a benchmark for liquidity and capital. Work towards that mark, and until you hit it, don't even think of holding property.

There is a point in time when you need write-offs, but that comes after this accumulation period.

◊ Create Contracts

In the real estate investment arena, where everybody is looking to benefit financially, it can create some very competitive situations. Unless you can read those predicaments, you can inexplicably hurt yourself and wind up with a financial loss. You want to avoid that type of situation at all costs.

The best transactions happen when there is mutual trust, where you understand the person who sits across the table as a potential team member with whom you're entering a partnership. The most efficient way to ensure all involved parties are clear on what is expected to provide and deliver is by creating a contract. By having everything spelled out in written form—most states do not allow for verbal agreements—creates a safeguard as you move forward in the process.

As a new investor, extended family members may come to you and ask for help in selling their home. You may want to get a start on your career and take on the purchase. Even though the trust is there, for the simple reason, you are family, get that contract created and signed into an agreement as quickly as feasible. Although there are no guarantees, listing steps, processes, benchmarks, and every little detail now can avoid bad blood down the road.

Here is a short reminder list of those with whom we create contracts.

- Buyer-seller
- Real estate agent
- Construction team
- Building inspectors

◊ Pay Attention to the Market

One of the factors that play the biggest part in your transaction decisions will be the cash flow—that monthly income (or working capital) versus the number of assets in your portfolio.

Whether you are the investor that buys and holds or the one that buys and sells, a lot depends on the market.

If you realize that the market is rapidly appreciating, hang on to the property for a little bit. But should you be in a stable market or declining market, then get rid of it. In the latter market types, you have nothing to gain by keeping the property.

Let's try to make this a bit clearer.

A property you own has a potential of an $80,000 profit margin. As the value appreciates at 5% year over year in a healthy market, that's a $4,000 increase. Now take that $80,000 and have it working for you in an investment program at 12 or 18%. In this case, you can then yield anywhere from $9,600 to over $14,000. That's a lot more return on your investment dollar.

People in real estate need to build wealth. That money materializes in more than one way. At the same time, and keep in mind, liquidity can come either from cash or assets.

However, should your assets have mortgages on them—most of them will—and the market goes south, declining quickly, those assets are gone. You are now stuck and may be one of those investors who sink and cannot recover.

The upside of a declining market is that if you build a certain amount of liquidity you can always capture other assets on the downturn.

Knowing where the market currently sits, what the history has been the past months, and being able to forecast activity, you, as a beginning investor has an advantage over someone who randomly buys and sells at will.

But how do you know the water is safe to dip your toe? This next section may help with your decision.

◊ 2007 Real Estate Crash – Why & How

You may remember an economic downturn a few years ago. The housing market did not fare well, and neither did some of those who had careers in real estate.

You are a bit worried and afraid that something like that would happen again. Could there be another crash like the one back in 2007?

Let me first talk about what I believed contributed to the collapse of the real estate market, and then circle back to the question if history might repeat itself.

Inflated Property Value

The price or value of a home is set down by real estate appraisers. They look at the property and evaluate the location, condition, and size. Their methods of evaluation seem to go in one direction only—up.

If a home were valued at $450,000 and sold at that same price, when ready to go on the market the next time, the appraisal would go up to $500,000 only because he may think if someone paid the $450,000 price tag, why wouldn't someone else pay the next step up?

The wayward thinking didn't stop there. Figuratively speaking, "If my house looks better than yours or is larger, and if someone got $500,000 for it, then you know I should get $550,000 for my house because it is in a better location!"

This unreasonable increasing of property values kept right on climbing higher and higher. "Yes. I want a pot of gold!"

The value of the property which was not congruent with its actual worth or supported by the substance of the real estate is my reason number one for the crash.

Greed

My second reason for the downfall is that, although the sellers were creating the behavior, the banks supported the frenzied activity. They saw an opportunity to cash in on the craziness.

The banks started creating programs to get people into homeownership to infuse even more money into the marketplace—the more money in circulation the more money that is made.

Mortgage programs—that engaged almost anybody with a heartbeat—began to develop.

Homeowners were needed to continue paying those higher prices, but the income they were receiving did not support the transaction. Therefore, lenders began to initiate something called the *stated-income program*.

"Okay. I'm just going to say that you have this amount of money as your yearly income, when in fact, you really don't."

The Collision

When a mortgage payment of $3,000 is put up against a total gross income of only $5,000, you know something has to give. Other financial obligations such as income taxes, insurance, food bills, and other expenses eat away at the amount of take-home pay. And so, the loosely created products and programs could not stand up against overvalued mortgages. People could not continue to meet the rising cost of housing based on a booming market. The two had to collide at some point.

Eventually, people want to survive and live their life. And that is when the brakes are applied.

"I know my house is important, but my family needs to eat. I need to afford the gas to go to work to pay the babysitter, too. I just can't continue paying this outrageous mortgage!"

BOOM!

The massive collapse occurs.

Will a Real Estate Crash Happen Again?

Even with the voracious finger pointing at the banks, property appraisers, real estate professionals—and even the owners who put their homes on the market, too—were all culpable. With all the evidence now in, the crash was not caused by one party.

A lot of what went wrong, however, is corrected. Much analysis has been done over these many years to put measures into place to divert this type of demise within the real estate market in the future.

Do I think that a crash could happen again? No one knows what the future holds. The one thing you can be sure of is that the real estate market, like other markets, are cyclical—they will rise or fall over time. Through your studies and by your practice in conjunction with your team of real estate professionals, you will be able to read the market, and successfully navigate the said market for consistent profits.

Now that you are aware of what happened in years past, you need not worry or be afraid of getting into the real estate arena. You possess the knowledge to keep your investing career in a safer environment as you grow into your future.

The Question Remains - Keep or Sell?

Since you have revisited your goals and know what to look for to avoid catastrophe as you enter the marketplace, you may have already decided what to do with the acquired property.

The bottom line is that the choice you make will affect your future decisions as a real estate investor.

Should you elect to hold onto the property for rental or other business income, then you make a choice to become a landlord or the owner of a different home for you and your family.

Should you elect to sell the acquired property and cash out your equity, then you will have a safety net for future acquisitions, or family and business emergencies.

You probably were hoping that I would give you the answer?

I cannot.

Your decision comes down to your initial, and overall goal—what you want to do that is consistent with your plan.

Summary

The answer to the big question of what to do with a property once it's ready to be disposed of could be one that occurs at the very beginning of the real estate investor process.

However, goals can change. The following checklist will help in your decision.

- Revisit goals
- Stick to the plan
- Build equity (in either case, if perceivable)

Notes & Review

This section is for your use to make note of any ideas that came to you while reading the chapter.

This section will also contain questions that were asked within the chapter concerning revisiting your goals. Space has been provided for you to record your answers.

1. Duration: Are you in for the long haul or short term?

_____

_____

_____

_____

2. Motivation: What is your natural stimulant, your why?

_____

_____

_____

_____

3. Aspiration: What do you wish to achieve?

_____

_____

_____

_____

4. Gratification: What are your strengths?

_____

_____

_____

5. Disinclination: What are your weakest points?

_____

_____

_____

Additional Notes

_____

_____

_____

_____

_____

_____

_____

9

The Disposition

The assumption is that you are leaning toward the real estate investor career by which property is purchased to turn a profit, and you plan on repeating the process as often as possible.

Therefore, and after carefully reviewing your goals for what you wish to accomplish by the end of the sale, let's take a look at the steps on how to get you there.

Choose a Real Estate Agent

To be the successful real estate investor you wish to be, you must have a credible team in place. One of the first people on that list should be a real estate agent. You may wonder why you need an agent at all. Are you not in the same business? Even though you are in the same industry, the answer to that question is a simple, "No."

Just as you need an accountant or lawyer as a partner on your team, so should you have a real estate agent. An agent can provide analysis and projections, and even do scouting and negotiations while you make use of your time and efforts in other ways.

You are seeking property to buy and sell. An agent is a person in the middle of the process. Therefore, you are the client of that emissary.

Select a few agents and get to know them, or rather, so they can get to know you and the type of property in which you are interested.

The decision to sell is then clear should you have several real estate agents who are feeding you—that is, directing to you—properties for your analysis and interests.

However, if you found the property on your own, you can decide on which real estate agent who will get the job to sell the property.

How should you pick an agent? The following criteria may be helpful.

◊ Market Knowledge

A person who has knowledge about the properties that are available or may become available is someone you want to know. You will also want that person (agent) to have the following:

- Skilled in accurately pricing properties within the area and dependent upon its condition
- Details about the asset for sale and familiarity with the frequency thereof
- Purchase resources in an area, along with a pre-approved list of clients with access to these resources

◊ Listing Proficiency

The number of listings an agent has may be a strong determinant of his efficiency in identifying and procuring assets for sale.

◊ Efficiency in the Quantitative and Qualitative Property Analysis Reports

The content and quality of the reports you receive from your real estate agent is a critical part of your decision-making process for a project completion timeline, ending with the sale date and sale price.

This information must be accurate and verifiable to be relied on and used by you. Errors in analysis or judgment could be costly. As an investor you would want to receive information from more than one source or agent to verify and validate the information—also known as intelligence—on which you base your decisions.

◊ Quality and Level of Service

If a practitioner/agent commits to supporting your business with accurate information promptly with a great attitude and professional service, this could be a good candidate for your team.

◊ Accessibility and Availability

In the real estate industry, as in life, things do not always go according to plan, to which may alter activity beyond our control, e.g., weather delays. Such occurrences can be costly, both in time and money.

Shifts in the marketplace due to political or economic pressures should be anticipated in the planning process, especially if they are likely to impact your transactions. Having access to a professional with knowledge about these factors—and one who is available to you on short notice—could significantly reduce your risk of loss, allowing for you to maintain profitability.

◊ Efficient Marketing Plan and Disposition System

An agent with a proven distribution plan—and a good list of potential buyers and sellers—is likely to be a good asset to your team. The agent's activity reflects, on a monthly basis, the efficiency—by those transactions—of his success rate.

◊ Adherence to Industry Best Practices

An agent who adheres to industry best practices puts protections in place and performs in such a manner as to reduce any risk or liability for their business or to your business. The agent will include these protections and best practices when writing up a plan for you.

◊ Who Found the Property

The expectation is to give the listing back to the agent who found the property for you in the first place. Continuing and keeping the relationship in good standing will be rewarding for you both—now and in the future.

For instance, Agent A found the perfect investment property. After the repairs have gone into fixing up the property you decide to list with Agent B. Unless you have good and just cause for not sticking with Agent A in giving him or her the listing, it stands to reason that Agent A will no longer be eager to find you great opportunities in the future.

Should you have found the property on your own, however, you can decide on the agent who meets other criteria, such as based on their past performance.

◊ Based on Performance

You, as the investor, must keep in mind there is no favoritism, just the facts in the execution of the sale. An agent's performance always has to do with numbers. And the bottom line contingency is you want an agent that will be able to move the property for you. Therefore, the real estate agent who has performed best would be awarded the property listing for sale—especially if you found the property on your own efforts.

Keep in mind that performance also may be defined in turnaround time. For example, the real estate agent has an exemplary record and history of completing sales within 30 days of a listing. That type of accomplishment should be added to the criteria when seeking your perfect real estate agent.

◊ Select Backup / Secondary Agent

There are advantages to having a few real estate agents in your back pocket. For starters, the more eyes you have out in the real estate arena who can be on the lookout for property that may be a good fit with your investing goals, the less time, perhaps, between transactions. You are then able to remain in a continual cash flow type of situation.

For instance, while Agent A is wrapping up the sale of one property, Agent B has found another property that fits your needs. You can begin working with Agent B and get the ball rolling on the next transaction.

Get Marketing Plan from Agent

Just as you contract with those who will complete the repairs and upgrades on a property, so should you secure an agreement from the real estate agent who will handle the listing. Should you decide along with your real estate agent that the listing is for a maximum of 90 days, then you will want to get a marketing plan that explains, in crisp detail what is involved.

It would also be a good time to get with one of your backup real estate agents to get an estimated plan. You won't want to get caught with a property that has no interest, much less an offer, 30 days after being listed. If that is the case, further examination must be performed to find where the downfall occurred. Agent A could have underestimated the time and overestimated the selling price, in which Agent B's estimated marketing plan may show that discrepancy. You can save yourself a lot of time and money ensuring you have both a marketing plan and a backup real estate agent.

But what types of items should be on the marketing plan you wonder?

◊ Fair Market Value Estimate

According to Wikipedia [https://en.wikipedia.org/wiki/Fair_market_value], "Fair market value (FMV) is an estimate of the market value of property, based on what a knowledgeable, willing, and unpressured buyer would probably pay to a knowledgeable, willing, and unpressured seller in the market."

Ask your real estate agents to give you an estimate of the fair market value of the property as it stands now and after repairs are complete.

If you know the property is listed at the best price, but even at this best price, doesn't receive lookers or bids in 30 days, consider the second, best price, as you want that property gone and out of your portfolio.

◊ Time to Sell Estimate

You want to have an agent who will move the property for you. Therefore, an important part of the marketing plan is for the real estate agent to offer an estimated time, in his or her opinion, as to how long you can expect to have the property on contract. And you will want to monitor this closely because time is money in the real estate investing business.

Let's say the agent has agreed to find a buyer in 90 days, providing the property is priced right. You took out a $300,000 loan at 12% interest per annum and, therefore, financing is costing you $36,000 for the year—or $3,000 a month. Because of the 90-day turnaround estimate, you budgeted for $9,000 in interest. Of course, it would be in your best interest to have that property gone as quickly as possible and spending $3,000 in interest is much better than $9,000.

But if the agent does not hold up to their estimate and cannot sell the property within the timeframe, you will be spending more than what you thought in interest, coming out of your net profit.

◊ Process & Methods to Sell Property

Along with the value and time estimates, the real estate agent should also include the procedural steps to dispose of the property. These would include how best the agent is going to market your asset and do specific actions at certain benchmarks to ensure a sale.

The process may look something like the following.

1. Submit property listing to MLS.
2. Create flyers for the property.
3. Electronically post, using the Internet and Social Media sites to promote the property.
4. Contact previous customers who were once interested in this type of assets.
5. Submit listing in local newspapers and magazines.
6. Schedule open house consistent with plans.

You may want the real estate agent to include clauses if the property does not sell within the first 30 days, 60 days, and 90 days so that you can get a feel for the agent's process and procedures as time marches on.

Below are examples of a clause.

- Within 60 days of initial listing, if the property not sold, 1) Lower the price, 2) Ramp up promotion, and so on.
- Within 90 days of initial listing, if the property is still not sold, 1) Re-examine the property, location, and anything else that which may be a hindrance to its selling, and 2) any other steps that make sense.

◊ Additional Methods to Sell Property

Another way to move your property quickly is to keep a For Sale sign on the property while it's being renovated. Curious visitors, as well as prospective purchasers, will often stop by to take a look, get general information, and express interest. At that time you could take their name and contact details either as a referral to your real estate agent or to handle the sale yourself, depending on your arrangements.

As a developer, many of the individuals with whom you work themselves are looking to become homeowners or investors. These too can become a pool of prospective buyers with whom you may be able to make great deals. Based on your financial position, including liquidity, these types of sales would support short term owner financing.

Another disposition process could be an auction with a reserve or a one-time open house with highest and best offers submitted at the time of viewing.

There are some psychological advantages associated with these two processes that will work in your favor and which include the spirit of competition and the created condition of scarcity. When these two are coupled with egos, you win.

In some slow markets, lease to own may also be an effective disposition strategy.

◊ Costs to Dispose of Property

Besides the methods the agent will use to dispose of the property, there will be advertising and other ad hoc costs. Some agents will include these costs as part of their process. Others will ask for an advertising budget to cover those costs.

Either way, ensure the marketing plan contains the costs to dispose of the property.

To Take the Sale or Not

There are some judgment calls that you have to make when an offer comes in on the property. For instance, the amount of money stated in the offer may come in lower than anticipated.

Even though you are disappointed, being flexible and willing to make adjustments may be the difference in making a sale or sitting with an unwanted piece of real estate for a few more months.

If you choose to stand your ground and hold out for a buyer who is willing to pay your asking price, you put yourself and perhaps your team at risk. You may need to re-evaluate the situation and take the hit to move onto the next property.

Let me explain a bit further.

◊ Lost Time

Once you receive an offer—which took some time for any movement to occur—and the yield is a lower-than-expected profit margin, you may be inclined to hold out for the price initially asked.

Retaining the attitude of knowing you can get your asking price might not be the best action step to do right now. If you choose to wait out the process and find someone who will pay your price, you could lose and waste time in the search for another property that may give a larger return or rather greater profit.

◊ Lost Money

Just as you may lose time in holding out for the person to come along and pay your price, you may lose money as well. The property has no value to you if you are sitting waiting for a buyer. Each day you sit, the interest on your loan is climbing. Each day you sit, another property that is out there somewhere goes untapped and unnoticed by you.

Again, re-evaluate your situation. The best decision you could make is to get rid of the property even if you have to take a reduction in the price.

With regards to disposition, it is perhaps better to take the lower price than to hold on and wait for a bigger offer, especially if the property has been on the market for more than 60 days.

Summary

You must remember that the profit stems from when you buy a property. The evaluation and analysis are done upfront so you can make the most from your investment. By having all the pieces and people in place, you will be able to make a wise decision to sell for profit or hold it for cash flow purposes when it comes to disposing of the property.

To help you make the best decision you need to:

- Determine the process and method for disposition of the property
- Choose a real estate agent that can list the property for you
- Get a marketing plan from the agent, so you are aware of the 30-60-90 day strategy and price point
- Know when to take the sale

Notes & Review

This section is for your use to make note of any ideas that came to you while reading the chapter.

This section will also contain questions that were asked within the chapter. Space has been provided for you to record your answers.

1. By what process will you dispose of the property?

_____

_____

_____

_____

_____

2. With what attributes will you choose a real estate agent to help you with the disposition of the property?

_____

_____

_____

_____

_____

3. What should a real estate agent include in the property
   disposal contract to ensure a smooth process?

_____

_____

_____

Additional Notes

_____

_____

_____

_____

_____

_____

_____

_____

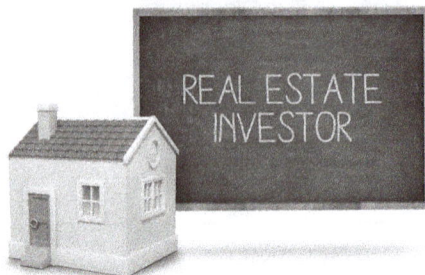

10

The Career

We already talked a lot in this book about real estate investing as a career. An entire chapter is devoted to your "big why" and the reasons behind looking into and ultimately choosing this pathway.

As with any career decision, you must examine your conscience to see if the opportunity is right for you. And if you have a family, you must decide if the choice is good for them as well.

Your Role and Responsibilities

If you choose to move ahead with the real estate investing career, be willing to give yourself and the process time to develop and adjust to get a sense and feel of the arena in which you have decided to play. It is also paramount and beneficial for you to work on developing the relationships necessary to succeed during this period.

◊ Choose to Be the Investor

If you approach it professionally, your job as a real estate investor is to work with your team to achieve the three components of a transaction:

1. Identify the property.

2. Fund the property.
3. See the property become a revenue source for lease or disposition.

Sounds easy, right? However, I know contractors and investors that try to do everything themselves, thinking that they are saving money. Let me tell you here and now they are not.

I'll put it in numbers.

First, let's consider the money. Contractor rates for a tiler, mason, or carpenter are around $50 an hour. As a real estate investor, you want to value your time anywhere between three and five hundred dollars an hour. Even if you split the profit with your agent, such as 60/40, you still come out way ahead in the numbers.

Next, let's consider the time involved. A real estate professional will spend anywhere from 40 to 60 hours marketing your property. By allowing the agent to do his or her job, you are free to spend your time at the highest and best use. Why spend the time sweating on construction or marketing when you can be looking for more property? Or better still, out having fun with friends or family!

Do not fix up real estate. Do not sell real estate. Your only job is to invest in real estate. Let the other professionals do the repairs, list, and complete the sale of the property. This process will make fewer headaches for you along your journey.

When you begin to pinch pennies think of it this way. While you are out and about doing your work or playing with your family, you put other people in the position to earn their living as they wish. You are adding to the betterment of your local economy, and improving lives at the same time.

"Highest and best use."

Highest and best use of land, highest and best use of property, highest and best use of your time.

You may ask, "What is the best use of my time?"

Only you can answer that question.

◊ Work Hard

You acknowledge that real estate investing is a tough and demanding business. You should also recognize, however, that it rewards and returns the energy you put into it. Any job does. Based on your practice, expectations, and experience, you ultimately decide what is best for you, and more importantly, what isn't.

Some new investors may have a complicated first transaction and decide this life is not for them. Other new investors will realize there is a learning curve. They are willing to keep going and work hard to gain the knowledge and experience necessary to become proficient.

You may have heard from someone that you can just jump into the world arena of real estate investing. You don't need to do any research; you don't need any training, but what is required to begin is the ability to obtain a huge loan on a property that allows you to fix it up and sell it in as little as 30 days for a substantial profit.

(You already know by reading this book that that is not how the process works.)

And so you find a piece of property in which to invest. That was easy enough. You are then able to secure a loan to do repairs. That was easy, too. But what begins to happen is that those repairs are not only taking longer than expected to complete, they also cost you more money than you have.

You are now frustrated, and the process begins to choke, leaving a bad taste in your mouth. Real estate investing may not be the career for you after all.

There are a few steps you can take to ensure this career will work for you.

1. Believe in yourself.
2. Find a mentor willing to walk through the process with you.
3. Complete at least three transactions from start to finish.

As in any career of choice, there is hard work involved—especially up front and as you begin the venture. This work also includes the need to learn and understand the language of the new business, plus the tricks and tips associated with the practice. Also be aware that not only is there work to be done on the practical application of real estate investing, but also where your positive mental attitude is concerned as well. That is the reason why believing in yourself is a first step in working hard to get what you want out of this business.

◊ Make Mistakes

Life, as a whole, can be complicated and challenging—as can be the life of a real estate investor. No one wants to make mistakes. However, mistakes can be a good lesson for learning. If you don't make some mistakes, learning can be limited. Sometimes a mistake may result in an improved outcome which gives a new direction for the future, although it began as an error or oversight.

Take for example the history of cheese. According to an ancient legend, it was made accidentally by an Arabian merchant who put his supply of milk into a pouch made from a sheep's stomach as he set out on a day's journey across the desert. The rennet in the lining of the bag, combined with the heat of the sun, caused the milk to separate into curd and whey. That night, the merchant found that the whey satisfied his thirst and the cheese (curd) had a delightful flavor, which satisfied his hunger.

Yes, I know food is not the same as a business career, but the idea behind it, of making mistakes—and lots of them—can lead to unimaginable and significant consequences in a good way.

There is something to be said regarding pressing through whatever challenges that may come your way and not letting life suck you in, so to speak. Let me share with you a story of a friend, James—which is not his real name—in his words.

~

James Shares His Story

Back in 2009, I had a number of properties. And with bursting bubbles and real estate at an all-time low, I was beyond clinically depressed. I would never kill myself because I could not do that to my family and friends but I really did not want to exist. I would wake up in the morning and be flooded with anxiety about what was to come that day. I was in a downward spiral.

At one point one of my best friends wanted to take me to Guatemala to get away. I had no money and could not see myself "vacationing" when I owed so much to so many. She insisted, and I conceded.

After a couple of days of being in Guatemala, I had a "what the heck is wrong with you" moment. I was stopped, waiting at a red light, when noticing a mother on the sidewalk, in a clown suit, juggling. The time was around 9 pm. I looked to the left, and I saw her young children on a stoop sleeping in someone's doorway. It was at that moment when realizing all of my "problems" were because I had signed my name on pieces of paper. This woman was juggling in a suit on a hot night to collect moneda so she could feed her family. It was truly a wake-up call.

Throughout my visit to Guatemala, we would pass a centrally located dump where people, and even children, would go through the trash to find things of use to bring back to what they called home. Examples of real problems kept presenting themselves to me.

My problems seemed so small and almost ridiculous when faced with the real and insurmountable problems I was witnessing. I promised myself that the next time I came back to Guatemala, I would try to help in some way.

Because it can get you from point A to point B, I am a firm believer in education. And since the knowledge and experience you obtain while learning—and of which can never be taken from you—I decided to focus my efforts on helping the school children of that country.

Upon coming back to the States, I was able to turn my real estate investing business around. After raising enough money to help the families of young children, I returned to Guatemala with the gathered resources. It didn't take much time for word to spread about what I was doing and, soon, however, I faced some tough decisions.

Even though deciding the funds raised would solely be for education and items associated with learning (uniforms, backpacks, school supplies), I was being asked to help particular families in need or to purchase medicines. Because I wasn't true to my mission or the goals that I set out to do, initially, I said no.

But, I'm human, and my heart ached by making that decision. I adjusted percentages to now include food and medicine, with the biggest percent remaining for education. Due to my fundraising efforts, I was fortunate and pleased to find out that some Guatemalan businesses would not be outdone by un Americano helping their people, much less in their country. Some donated books while other businesses donated medicine.

Clearly, a win-win situation for all.

So, when asked why I do what I do for the children and their country, my response is, "Well, in a nutshell, Guatemala saved my life."

~

Just think. One night James had the epiphany that turned his circumstances completely around when, just a couple days before, he was "beyond clinically depressed."

You don't want ever to get into a situation like James, but his story exemplifies that no matter how dire things look, change for the better is always at hand—your hand. Don't worry about the mistakes you make. Focus on how you can do better, so they don't happen again.

◊ Invest in Yourself

You may have come to this book as someone wanting to explore the real estate investing arena. You may be here as someone who has dabbled in the field, made a few mistakes, wanting to know where you went wrong, and wish to improve your process. You may also be a person who knows of someone in the business that has lost the interest in the real estate investing process and you want to know how you can avoid losing steam inside your career.

Let me say that you are in the right place. You took the first correct step to ensure your success as a real estate investor by buying this book. You are excited about this new adventure, but knew you needed to understand the full picture. You want to make sure you get off on the right foot.

I knew a gentleman who lost passion for this work. I suggested on numerous occasions that George (not his real name) obtain counsel or get assistance to return to his game. George's distaste for the real estate investing world grew over time, yes, but primarily because he did not receive proper training in the beginning to ensure his success. And he refused any help later.

George kept on with his routine of finding the property, getting only one repair estimate—and that was from a friend—which often was inaccurate. Soon George would realize the repairs were more than the estimate, losing money. Unwilling to invest in a coaching or mentoring program, George gave up and gave in to the frustration.

There's a lot of inherent risks of which sole or new investors need to be aware. Aren't knowing those risks worth the price of hiring a coach or mentor to be trained on what to look for when starting out? Of course, it's worth the cost!

Can you imagine a surgeon operating on someone without knowing how to do the procedure? The example may be extreme, but yet one of the same complexity.

To be effective as a real estate investor, you must invest in yourself and the process. Just as it is with any job, unless you have training about the processes and tasks involved, you risk being unsuccessful, the occupation itself will leave a bad taste in your mouth; you become disgruntled, and you could end up like George, looking for another career.

When you hire the assistance of a coach or mentor, somebody that has done the work, made the mistakes, been successful, you are more likely to thrive in the business.

As you enter the world of real estate investing, there is a real case for adding this education piece to your budget. The cost of programs vary as much as the information inside them. Do your due diligence when selecting a person from whom you want to learn.

And one last thing. Don't worry about the cost. Your investment will return through the profits received on the transactions you make.

Summary

As you move forward from this point, take the time necessary to make the right decision for you and your family when selecting your next career, be it the real estate investor or some other choice.

Remember, when your decision is choosing this as a career you must:

- Choose it
- Work hard at it
- Make mistakes and learn from them
- Invest in yourself

Notes & Review

This section is for your use to make note of any ideas that came to you while reading the chapter.

This section will also contain questions that were asked within the chapter. Space has been provided for you to record your answers.

1. What is the easiest piece in choosing to become a real estate investor?

_____

_____

_____

_____

2. What would be the one thing to stop you from seeing REI as a career?

_____

_____

_____

_____

3. Who will be on your list or go-to person to help you train and gain experience as an investor?

_____

_____

_____

_____

Additional Notes

_____

_____

_____

Epilogue

Will I Commit to the Process and Do the Work?

"I see real estate investing as a career and as my primary income stream."

I like to say everybody can do the work of a real estate investor. However, you have to determine if you are an "everybody."

Although the interest is there, you just can't start by randomly looking at properties. You also cannot do an eyeball evaluation to conclude the property will yield a profit.

You must first figure out the costs involved, such as repairs or the interest on money borrowed, and including the purchase price. Forecasting is the next step on what the returns are going to be after all is said and done.

There is a lot of work, both physical and mental, which goes into each transaction. After the legwork, you may find that the property may not be worth your time and effort. Would this be a disappointment? Would you be discouraged in seeking out another property in which to invest?

How you handle this type of experience can make or break you as an investor. If you look back on the steps and find the one or two pieces that went wrong or weren't just right, you can learn from that experience. You will either not make the same mistake again, or tweak the process to accommodate the gap in judgment.

If you document the whole process the first time going through, all the steps and actions, what the experience was like, how you feel at a certain point in time about the project, and how it impacted your family, can be most helpful.

Once you do three, four, or five complete transactions, and have your team together, the process gets easier, and you start to see the benefit.

But it all depends on you.

Everybody can live a wonderful and happy life, but not everybody wants to. I think it's a matter of choice. And if you choose to do the work, then you should ostensibly get the right knowledge or foundation on which to build and develop this type of a career.

What am I willing to commit to in becoming a real estate investor?

A. Time
B. Research
C. Documenting process
D. Patience

Moving Forward

There is a decision forthcoming and on the horizon. You may have all the information necessary to go forward, or you may decide that you need to make further inquiries.

Either way, you will move forward.

I firmly believe that by talking with someone who has accomplished investment transactions is a good next step. Assessing whether or not to proceed as a real estate investor with another investor who can guide you and help allay fears that can keep you from a career you are, perhaps, meant to have.

You may be itching to get out into the arena, break into a sprint and get started, but the process is one where you must first learn how to walk before you run. You must know how to balance yourself when standing alone.

Anyone can be a real estate investor. However, you have to know what you are doing and how to work through the process the right way, by taking the proper steps.

If you should choose to move forward and learn the ropes of real estate investing, I highly recommend working with someone in person. Stay away from on-line training, such as you would find on YouTube, unless of course, your mentor has his or her training hosted on that website.

When it comes to practical experience, you need someone who will be there to show you, hands-on. You want to be in-person when looking at a mainframe of a house, warped paneling, or leaky pipes to learn and discern issues for that property and that of those to come in the future.

Sometimes you encounter individuals who would like you to believe that they know everything about everything. And then there are those who know a little about many things. These two types of individuals can sometimes sound the same. You must learn to separate the ones who possess genuine knowledge and insight—and can help you to succeed—from those who only pretend to have the knowledge. As one young lady, who just purchased a home, said, "Don't confuse my nursing degree with your knowledge from Google search."

As you move forward from this point, take the time necessary to make the right decision for you and your family.

Join My Team

One of the reasons for writing this book was to share the truth with people like you who are interested in real estate investing as a career. After seeing many gurus out there who hold huge in-person conventions to gain new investors and how they are more interested in the dollars that they get into their own pockets, I was compelled to show the genuine side of REI.

You owe it to yourself and your family to get the best training and mentoring money can buy—and at an affordable price!

You've read about the Shared Equity Program I offer. We will work together to ensure you get a full understanding of the entire process of investing—from the point of looking for property, gathering your team, obtaining financing, all the way to depositing your profits into your bank account.

To learn more about how you can thrive as a real estate investor, let's have a conversation. Connect with me at RCPHIPPS@ GMAIL. COM or call (617) 296-7730.

I look forward to working with you.

About the Author

Richard C. Phipps, a committed and qualified Real Estate Broker, licensed in Massachusetts, with over 35 years of experience in many areas of the real estate industry. He is an undisputed industry visionary and leader, with a passion to provide home ownership opportunities through education and training. He has extensive knowledge, education and experience in real estate law, personal and corporate tax law, foreclosure prevention and financial planning. His licenses included: Series 6, 63 and 26, Life and Health, Real Estate Broker and Instructor. Current and prior boards of advisory include, Barbadian Cultural Committee of Boston, Action for Boston Community Development, Mattapan Hyde Park Economic Development Corporation., National Association of Real Estate Brokers, and his hobbies include hosting at Boston Neighborhood Network and Toastmasters International.